EXPLORE MAKERSPACE!

Alicia Klepeis
Illustrated by Matt Aucoin

More science titles in the **Explore Your World!** Series

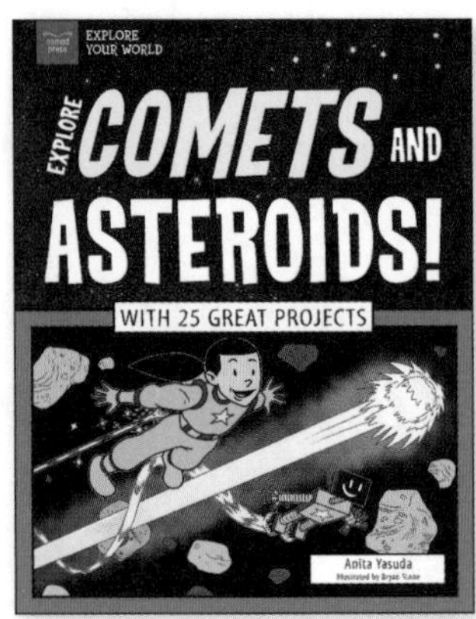

Check out more titles at www.nomadpress.net

Nomad Press
A division of Nomad Communications
10 9 8 7 6 5 4 3 2 1

This book was manufactured by Versa Press,
East Peoria, Illinois
September 2017, Job #J17-06358

ISBN Softcover: 978-1-61930-566-3
ISBN Hardcover: 978-1-61930-562-5

Educational Consultant, Marla Conn

Questions regarding the ordering of this book should be addressed to
Nomad Press
2456 Christian St.
White River Junction, VT 05001
www.nomadpress.net

Printed in the United States of America.

CONTENTS

Interested in primary sources? Look for this icon.
Use a smartphone or tablet app to scan the QR code and explore more! You can find a list of URLs on the Resources page.

If the QR code doesn't work, try searching the Internet with the Keyword Prompts to find other helpful sources.

KEYWORD PROMPTS

makerspace

TIMELINE

Since the beginning of time, people have been makers. They have created tools, buildings, clothing, vehicles, works of art, and more. This timeline covers engineers and makers from ancient times to modern-day makerspaces. While makerspaces can be found in nations around the world, this timeline is focused mainly on those the United States.

ABOUT 2550 BCE: The ancient Egyptian Imhotep is sometimes referred to as the first documented engineer. He is known for designing, and likely supervising, the construction of the Pyramid of Djoser, located in Saqqara, Egypt.

THIRD CENTURY BCE: The Greek scientist Archimedes creates a screw machine to pump water.

FIRST CENTURY BCE: The Roman military engineer and architect Vitruvius writes *De Architectura*, a 10-volume work on machines, buildings, science, and architecture. Some describe this work as "a guide for building projects."

1700S CE: The first schools of engineering are founded. One example is the National School of Bridges and Highways, which opened in France in 1747.

1863: Willard Gibbs is awarded the first PhD in engineering in the United States, from Yale University.

1905: Frances Jenkins Olcott, the children's department head at the Carnegie Library of Pittsburgh, Pennsylvania, organizes crafts such as basketry and sewing for kids visiting the library.

1979: The newly expanded Merrimack Public Library in New Hampshire opens with a kids' craft room.

1985: The MIT Media Lab is founded at Massachusetts Institute of Technology in Massachusetts. Research groups here work on projects ranging from wearable computers to electric cars.

MID-1990S: The Geek Group in Michigan and c-base in Germany form hackerspaces, where members can use equipment and facilities to work on individual and collaborative technology projects.

2003: The MIT Center for Bits and Atoms works to encourage the development of fab labs (fabrication laboratories) in cities and rural communities around the world. Fab labs often include equipment such as a 3-D printer, laser cutter, electronics workbench, and more.

APRIL 2006: The first Maker Faire is held in California. This event celebrates engineering, science projects, arts and crafts, and the do-it-yourself community.

APRIL 2009: Maker Bot, one of the earliest desktop 3-D printers, is available for sale.

2011: The Fayetteville Free Library Makerspace opens in Fayetteville, New York. It is the first U.S. public library to install a permanent makerspace. The space includes a 3-D printer.

MAY 2014: The White House launches the Mayors Makers Challenge to support makers at the local level. It also hosts the first White House Maker Faire.

2016: There are nearly 1,400 makerspaces around the world. That's 14 times more makerspaces than there were in 2006.

shingles
sod
decipher
suspension bridge
programming
sloped
obstacle
structure
hull
Middle Ages
invention
cargo
laser
dense
binary code
axle
armor
concept
bridge
principle
method
technology
grid
engineering
prototype
device
objective
sound
wave
makerspace
Hertz
computer
pitch
mass
tinker
buoyancy
strategy
engineer
collaborate
data
system
calculation
climate
collage
liquid
abacus
automatic
efficient
thatch

INTRODUCTION

WHAT IS A MAKERSPACE?

Cardboard tubes. Building blocks. Scissors and paper. Have you ever used these materials to create something new? Then you are a maker!

People around the globe invent, create, and build things every day. One day you might use Lego bricks to build a house. The next day you might use those same plastic bricks to make something completely different, such as a truck or a plane. The process of creating and building is sometimes called "making" or "tinkering." People often do this kind of activity in makerspaces, where there are plenty of supplies to choose from.

WORDS TO KNOW

tinker: to adjust or repair something in an experimental manner.

makerspace: a work space inside a library, school, or other place where people can work together to make, explore, and learn using tools of all kinds.

computer: an electronic device that stores and processes information.

device: a piece of equipment, such as a phone, that is made for a specific purpose.

engineering: the use of science and math in the design and construction of machines and structures.

design: to make a sketch or plan.

structure: something that is built, such as a building, bridge, tunnel, tower, or dam.

engineer: a person who uses science, math, and creativity to design and build things.

concept: an idea.

WORDS TO KNOW

Many of the things you build or make can be created in your home, but other projects might require more complex tools or supplies. What if you want to create a robot that moves? Or a solar-powered car? Or a new computer game? You might want to go to a makerspace to work on projects such as these.

ARE YOU AN ENGINEER?

Engineering is a type of science that is concerned with designing and building machines, roads, ships, buildings, and many other types of structures. People who work in engineering are called engineers. They use science, math, and creativity to design products or processes that meet human needs or solve problems.

When you tinker in a makerspace, you are working with the same types of tools and scientific concepts that engineers work with on their jobs!

collaborate: to work with others.

WORDS TO KNOW

DIFFERENT MAKERSPACES

There are makerspaces all around the United States. Some are in schools and libraries. Others are in museums. They are even found in people's homes. Large or small, makerspaces are great places to create, tinker, and learn.

People of all ages can collaborate, or work together, on projects in makerspaces. You can also work on your own project in a makerspace.

DID YOU KNOW?

In the 1970s, Steve Wozniak tinkered as a member of the Bay Area's Homebrew Computer Club. He invented the Apple-1 computer in 1976. In 2014, this Apple-1 computer sold for $905,000.

THE FIRST MAKERSPACE

The first modern makerspace in a public library was created at the Fayetteville Free Library in New York in 2011. A woman named Lauren Smedley was in graduate school when she came up with the idea of putting a 3-D printer into a library and creating a space where people could come and build things. The library's director thought that was an excellent idea and hired Smedley to make it happen! Now, the Fayetteville Free Library calls its makerspace a fab lab. It's a place where anyone can come and use the materials, get ideas, and collaborate with other people!

milling machine: a machine that can cut or carve different materials.

laser: a device that generates an intense beam of light. Lasers are often used in cutting and drilling, playing CDs, and even for surgery.

WORDS TO KNOW

The popularity of makerspaces has grown a lot during the past 10 years. Sometimes, people use different terms to describe makerspaces. Here are just a few of them.

FAB LABS: These makerspaces provide access to lots of modern tools for invention. Milling machines allow people to cut or carve materials such as metal and wood. They can drill, make slots, and even create perfectly square corners on something. Laser cutters use a beam of light to cut through many different materials. People can use these tools to make jewelry or holiday ornaments, for example. Fab labs have many other kinds of equipment as well. At a fab lab, it's possible to create almost anything!

TECH SHOPS: People pay to join these makerspaces. Here, members can get access to industrial tools and equipment, such as sewing machines, 3-D printers, and woodworking and welding machines.

DID YOU KNOW?

Some libraries let you check out more than just books and movies. Sewing machines and a handy person to help with chores are two things you might be able to check out of a library!

There is a lot of advice on the Internet about creating makerspaces in your home! **Check out this article for some great ideas.**

KEYWORD PROMPTS

programming: to give a computer a set of step-by-step instructions that tells it what to do.

digital art: art created using computers.

WORDS TO KNOW

HACKERSPACE: Sometimes called "hacklabs," these makerspaces are often focused on computer programming and digital art. People here might work to put computer parts together to make new devices.

SETTING UP YOUR MAKERSPACE

You might have been to a makerspace in your school or library. You can also create your own makerspace at home! You don't need lots of fancy, high-tech equipment to get started. After all, a makerspace is simply a place to create and play while solving problems and answering questions.

You might be lucky enough to have space in your house to dedicate as a makerspace. That way you can leave your supplies set up. You can also create a portable makerspace in a box or other container that you can close up and put away whenever you're done inventing.

bridge: a structure built over something, such as a river or road, so that people can cross.

method: a way to do something.

WORDS TO KNOW

Here is a list of items to get you started. Don't worry if you only have some of them. There's no perfect makerspace—only great ideas!

* rubber bands
* glue
* stapler with staples
* tape (masking, packing, scotch)
* cardboard
* tissue paper
* paper plates
* paper of all colors and kinds (magazines, newspapers, old cards)
* crayons, paints, markers
* recycled items (plastic bottles, takeout containers, scraps of wood)
* ribbons, string, embroidery thread, fabric scraps
* plastic garbage bags
* twist-ties from garbage bags
* bubble wrap
* pipe cleaners
* popsicle sticks, straws
* wire hangers, craft wire
* building sets, such as Legos, wood blocks, tinker toys

HELPFUL HINT: If you want additional supplies, the dollar store or a local craft shop is likely to have whatever you have in mind.

In *Explore Makerspace!*, you'll learn many different engineering concepts. For example, you'll learn how buildings and bridges stay standing, how music travels through the air, and why boats float (and sink!). You'll also explore different methods people use to make art and create games. You'll do lots of activities that will let you explore these different concepts, and have tons of fun, too!

ENGINEERING DESIGN PROCESS

Every engineer keeps a notebook with the details of the engineering design process. As you read through this book and do the activities, keep track of your observations, data, designs, and prototypes in an engineering design worksheet, like the one shown here. When doing an activity, remember that there is no right answer or right way to approach a project. Be creative and have fun!

Each chapter of this book begins with an essential question to help guide your exploration of engineering.

Problem: What problem are we trying to solve?

Research: Has anything been invented to help solve the problem? What can we learn?

Question: Are there any special requirements for the device? An example of this is a car that must go a certain distance in a certain amount of time.

Brainstorm: Draw lots of designs for your device and list the materials you are using!

Prototype: Build the design you drew during brainstorming.

Test: Test your prototype and record your observations.

Evaluate: Analyze your test results. Do you need to make adjustments? Do you need to try a different prototype?

? INVESTIGATE!

What problem do you see that you would like to fix? What can you invent to solve it?

Keep the question in your mind as you read the chapter. At the end of each chapter, use your engineering notebook to record your thoughts and answers.

WORDS TO KNOW

data: information in the form of facts and numbers.

prototype: a working model that lets engineers test their idea.

PROJECT!

MAKERSPACE JOURNAL

Both engineers and scientists keep track of many things. They write down observations about what they see around them and questions they have as they work on projects. Scientists record the steps they take each time they work on a scientific project, while engineers write down the changes they make to their inventions. Create a special journal or notebook to help you keep track of the makerspaces you visit both in person and on the Internet and what you observe or work on there.

SUPPLIES

* 5–10 sheets lined paper
* 5–10 sheets blank paper
* stapler or paper clip
* art supplies (markers, crayons, colored pencils)
* pencil
* camera or computer printer (optional)

1 Find out if there are any makerspaces located in your town or not too far away. You can ask your local school or public librarian for advice. Ask an adult for help using the Internet to research places you might be able to visit.

2 Stack your pages with lined sheets between unlined sheets so you have a mix of both. Make sure the bottom sheet is unlined. Fold the stack in half with the unlined sheet on the outside. Staple down the middle of the pages to make a notebook. Write your name on the front cover and decorate it. This is your design journal!

WHY ARE LIBRARIES SO TALL?
Because of all the stories.

PROJECT!

3 Each time you visit a makerspace, create a two-page spread about it. You can include the chart below to keep your observations organized. It's fine to do a virtual visit—you can look at lots of great makerspaces online.

4 For each makerspace, create a sketch of what it looks like. You can also paste a photo in your design journal.

Name of Makerspace	Location (City/State)	Library, Museum, School, or Other Setting	Tools Available	Types of Projects You Saw

THINK ABOUT IT: Which makerspaces did you like best? Why? Remember to consider both the ones you saw in person and those you visited online. What kinds of projects did you get to work on? Were there any tools you wish the makerspace had? What designs did you come up with while you were there?

PROJECT!

DESIGN YOUR OWN MAKERSPACE

In this activity, you can design your ultimate makerspace. It could be a big one like in a school or library or a compact one in your house. Dream big!

SUPPLIES

- paper or posterboard
- pencil
- markers
- computer (optional)

1 Brainstorm about all of the kinds of projects you'd like to be able to work on in your ideal makerspace. Make a list of the tools that you might need to work on these projects.

2 With an adult's permission, you can look online to see some examples of makerspaces. A simple Google search of "makerspace designs" turns up many images of these places.

3 Using a pencil, sketch out your design. Be sure to include spaces for tools, for people to work, and so on.

4 When you are satisfied with your makerspace, color in your design. Imagine that you have no limits on your budget. Have fun with color, tools, etc.

5 Share your creation with your friends, teachers, or librarians.

TRY THIS! Could you make a 3-D model of your makerspace? What materials would you use? Why would this be helpful in planning a real makerspace?

CHAPTER 1

EXCITING ENGINEERING

When you make structures from cardboard tubes or build towers from blocks, you are using the same skills engineers use when they design buildings made from wood and steel!

While engineers don't build actual structures, such as bridges and buildings, in a makerspace, they might use a makerspace to build a model of the real structure. While they are designing, engineers need to think about the materials they will use. Using materials with enough strength is important. Engineers might try different materials to find the ones that work just right.

invention: an original process or device.

technology: the tools, methods, and systems used to solve a problem or do work.

system: a group of objects or parts that work together.

WORDS TO KNOW

? INVESTIGATE!

Why do engineers and designers strive to improve products used in our daily lives? Why do we use the engineering design process to solve design challenges?

Engineers are people who design and build different kinds of machines and structures. Do you enjoy making devices work better? Do you like to solve problems or build things? Then you might enjoy working as an engineer.

Sometimes, the way engineers can turn their ideas into new inventions and designs might seem like magic. But in reality, engineers use science and technology to solve practical problems.

There are many different kinds of engineers. Civil engineers design roads and other types of transportation systems. Mechanical engineers design all kinds of machines, including elevators, air-conditioning systems, and the engines in your cars.

Electrical engineers design everything from computers and robots to systems that deliver electricity to your school or home. Aerospace engineers work on airplanes, jets, and rocket ships.

CROSSING BRIDGES

Imagine you are walking through a forest on your way to a friend's house. The house is many miles away. Suddenly, you come to a raging river. What do you do?

This type of situation has challenged lots of people, including famous explorers, for as long as humans have been on the move! One solution to this problem is to walk to the end of the river and continue walking on dry land. But that could take a long time. Another solution? Build a bridge!

THE ZHAOZHOU BRIDGE

The Zhaozhou Bridge is the oldest standing bridge in China. Sometimes called the "King of Bridges," it is located in the Hebei Province in northeastern China. This stone bridge was built more than 1,400 years ago, during the Sui Dynasty. It took 10 years to build and is 167 feet long and 31 feet wide. The Zhaozhou Bridge has survived eight wars, 10 floods, and numerous earthquakes. And it still carries people across the Jiaohe River! Look at the structure of the bridge. What characteristics do you spot that have helped it stay standing for so long?

ravine: a small narrow valley with steep sides.

obstacle: something that blocks a person's way or stops progress.

Inca: the South American people who built a great empire in the Andes Mountains 800 years ago.

suspension bridge: a bridge that has its roadway suspended from two or more cables that are strongly anchored at the ends.

WORDS TO KNOW

A bridge is a structure that continues a road, path, or railroad across a river, ravine, or other obstacle. Bridges have been around since ancient times. People often constructed early bridges from logs or other materials that were easy to find, such as rocks.

The Incas of South America were master bridge builders. They made ropes from twisted mountain grass and other plants. Then they constructed simple suspension bridges from these ropes and stretched them across deep ravines.

Many modern-day bridges are made from steel. This is a strong, light metal. As technology improves, engineers can design longer and stronger bridges. The Danyang-Kunshan Grand Bridge in China is more than 102 miles long and runs between two cities, Shanghai and Nanjing. Spain even has a bridge called the Alamillo that looks like a harp!

sloped: a surface that has one end or side that is at a higher level than the other.

shingles: rectangular tiles that cover a roof or the sides of a building. Shingles can be made of wood, metal, asphalt, or other material.

thatch: a plant material, such as straw, used to cover the roofs of buildings.

climate: the weather patterns in an area during a long period of time.

WORDS TO KNOW

LOOK UP!

Engineers also design buildings. One part of the building an engineer thinks about carefully is the roof.

Roofs can be flat or sloped. They can be covered in shingles or metal. There are all different kinds of roofs. Around the world, they are built differently, for different purposes. For example, traditional homes in Africa might have thatch roofs made of straw or palm leaves.

PERSON 1:
DID YOU CROSS THAT HUGE BRIDGE?
Person 2:
Yeah, but I still can't get over it!

One reason there are different types of roofs is that different materials are available around the world. Another reason is the climate where the roof is built. You wouldn't want a roof that allows the breeze to get through in a cold place like northern Canada, would you?

pitch: the steepness of a slope, particularly of a roof.

collapse: to fall in or down suddenly.

WORDS TO KNOW

Engineers also have to think about the pitch of a roof. In some parts of the country, you'll see flat roofs. In other areas, you'll see steep roofs.

Do you live in an area that gets a lot of snow? What happens to the roof during a heavy snowstorm? If too much snow builds up on the roof, it might be in danger of collapsing. If the roof has a steep pitch, the snow can slide off onto the ground!

Engineers think about all of these things when they design bridges and houses. When you are working on smaller projects in your makerspace, how do you decide what type of bridge to build or what pitch the roof of a structure should be?

In the next chapter, we'll learn more about technology, electricity, computers, and different technology projects you can do in your makerspace!

CONSIDER AND DISCUSS

It's time to consider and discuss: Why do engineers and designers strive to improve products used in our daily lives? Why do we use the engineering design process to solve design challenges?

PROJECT!

BUILD A BRIDGE

What bridges do you cross where you live? Bridges can be made of steel, cement, wood, or even logs placed across a stream. Depending on the materials you use, your bridge will be stronger or weaker. In your makerspace, can you create a bridge that can support the weight of five toy cars or five building blocks? Use the engineering design process to organize your work.

SUPPLIES

* engineering notebook
* twist-ties from garbage bags
* paper clips
* pipe cleaners
* string or twine
* toy cars or building blocks
* boxes or cardboard tubes

1 Figure out how long the bridge needs to be to fit five cars or blocks across it.

2 In your engineering notebook, create a sketch of what you want your bridge to look like. Decide what you think would be good supports for the four corners of the bridge. How will you attach the bridge to these supports? What will you use to build the bottom, or roadway, of the bridge?

3 Using twist-ties, pipe cleaners, or whatever materials you choose, build the base of the bridge. Attach the base to the supports.

4 One at a time, place your cars or blocks onto the bridge. Does it break? How many weights can your bridge hold?

THINK ABOUT IT: Did your first design work? How can you make your bridge stronger? How can you make it more flexible? What other materials can you use? Try to make different bridges and see if you can make them stronger!

PROJECT!

LOOK OUT FOR SNOW

SUPPLIES

- plastic garbage bag
- cardboard box or shoebox
- tape
- scissors
- cardboard, thick paper, thin metal, Styrofoam, or other material
- at least 1½ cups of glitter, sand, or soap flakes (like Ivory) for snow

From Washington State to Vermont, there are many places in the United States that get snow during the winter. Snow in the western part of the United States tends to be drier and lighter and less dense than the snow on the East Coast. If there is too much snow on a roof, it can cause problems for homeowners. The roof could even cave in! Also, if snow melts and refreezes, it can form ice dams that can cause leaks or other water damage. Can you design a roof that makes it easy for snow to fall off?

1 Place a garbage bag in the area where you will do your experiment. This will make cleanup easier!

2 Decide which box will be your house. A shoebox standing upright is an easy choice.

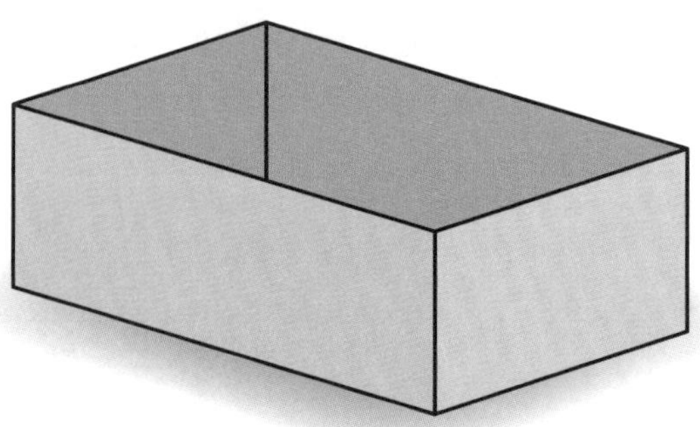

3 Gather your different roofing materials in one place. You can cut or bend the material to the size and angle you want.

WORDS TO KNOW

dense: how tightly the matter in an object is packed.

matter: anything that has weight and takes up space.

ice dam: a wall of ice that forms on the edge of a roof that can cause water damage.

PROJECT!

4 Choose one material to start. Put the material flat onto the house. You may need to lightly tape the roof on so it doesn't slip off with the "snow."

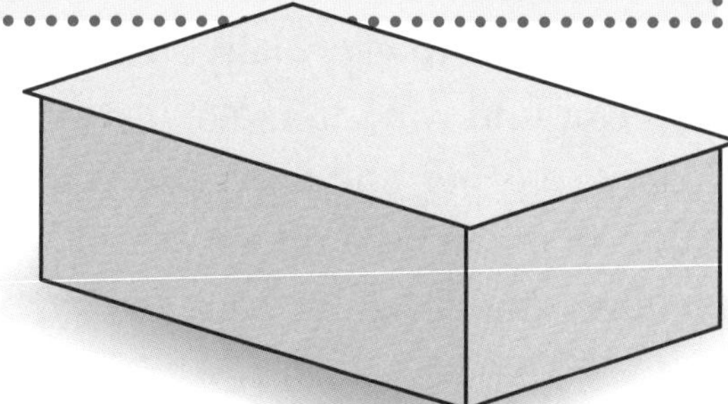

5 Pour ½ cup of snow onto the flat roof. What happens?

6 Use the same roofing material, but move the roof to a steeper pitch on the house. Pour the snow on again. What happens? Was a flat or slanted roof easier for the snow to fall off? Which would you choose to use in a snowy location?

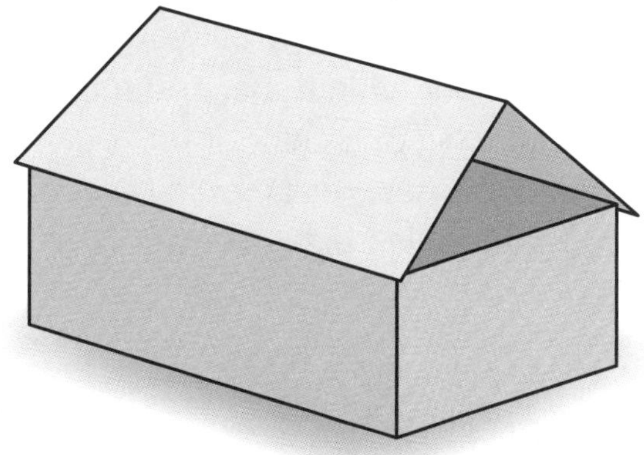

DID YOU KNOW?

In the book *Little House on the Prairie*, the Ingalls family lives in a house with a sod roof, which is a roof made of dirt and grass.

TRY THIS! Try this same experiment again with different types of roofing materials, such as corrugated cardboard and aluminum foil. Which roof was hardest or easiest for the snow to fall off? Why? Are there things you can do to these materials to make them more slippery for snow?

WORDS TO KNOW

sod: the grass-covered surface of the ground.

PROJECT!

SUPER STRONG NEWSPAPER

Many people enjoy reading the newspaper. But have you ever used it as a building material? It might not seem especially strong at first, but you can find ways to make it stronger. Using just newspaper and tape, can you build a small table that can hold up a stack of books? Use the engineering design process to organize your work.

SUPPLIES

- lots of newspaper
- pen or pencil
- scissors
- ruler
- tape—masking, packing, or scotch
- books or other heavy objects

1 On a piece of newspaper, trace a square that is 12 inches by 12 inches.

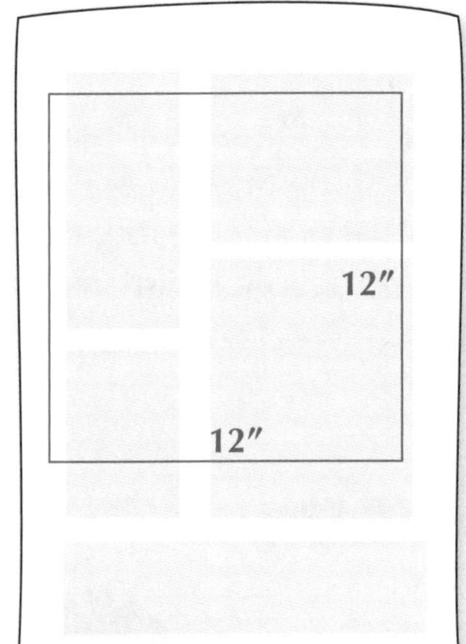

2 Think about how tall you want your table to be. You might want to sit in a chair or on your couch to see what would be a comfortable height for your table.

3 Before using any tape, experiment with different techniques for getting your newspaper to be the right height. Folding or rolling newspapers are two examples of ways to gain height. You can also make layers of newspaper and tape them together.

4 Using just your tape and newspaper, build your table.

PROJECT!

5 When you are done building, see how many books you can pile on top of the table without it breaking.

THINK ABOUT IT: Can you think of other materials you could use to make your structure stronger? How many books did your table support before it broke?

TRY THIS! You can use newspaper to build a cubby house! By rolling the newspaper tightly and sealing each roll with tape, you can make long narrow tubes. These tubes can form the "bones" of the house. You can make it as wide and as tall as you want. When you're done with the basic structure, use a sheet for a roof. How much newspaper do you need to make your house strong enough for a roof? What are some other materials you could use?

WOMEN ARE ENGINEERS, TOO

When you read about the history of engineering, you might think only men worked in these jobs. There were women, too, but they are often overlooked in the history books! Emily Warren Roebling (1843–1903) is known as the first female field engineer. Her husband was the head engineer for the Brooklyn Bridge project, but he became very sick during the construction and had to stay in bed. Roebling traveled to the building site almost every day and made important decisions about what needed to be done and how. She was also the first person to cross the bridge by carriage—she carried a rooster with her as a sign of victory!

CHAPTER 2

TERRIFIC TECHNOLOGY

Every day you use technology. You talk on the phone, watch television, listen to the radio, and use the Internet. Even the family car runs on technology! What other forms of technology do you use every day?

Technology is fun to work with in your makerspace. If you have a computer, you can work on learning coding. You can also explore older types of technology, such as an abacus or wheels!

? INVESTIGATE!

How can technology and the engineering design process benefit us in solving problems in our daily lives?

Sometimes, the technology you use can be complicated, such as when you need to get an X-ray at the hospital or are playing a virtual reality game. Other times, technology is simple, such as ringing the doorbell so that a friend knows you've arrived at their house.

What exactly *is* technology? Technology is the use of tools, methods, and systems to solve a problem or do work. When people use science to solve problems, they are using technology.

DID YOU KNOW?

Normally, people blink about 15 to 22 times each minute. When people are using a computer, they only blink about seven times per minute!

For example, people like to be able to communicate with each other wherever they are in the world. To solve the problem of how to communicate when one person is in the United States and the other person is in South Africa, engineers have invented many devices and methods through the years. Some of these inventions include telephones, email, and FaceTime. These are all types of technology that let people talk to and/or see each other despite the great distances between them.

COMPUTERS AND CODING

Computers are a big part of technology today. People use them for work, entertainment, and education. Computers help us solve problems. There are computers at the doctor's office, at school, and even at the grocery store.

For many people, computers are an essential part of everyday life. They allow people to manage large amounts of information.

abacus: an instrument for performing calculations by sliding beads along rods.

calculation: a mathematical determination of the number or size of something.

principle: the basic way that something works.

automatic: working with little or no direct control by people.

WORDS TO KNOW

It might seem hard to imagine, but the history of the computer began more than 2,500 years ago! The abacus is an invention from the Middle East. An abacus is basically a simple calculator. Made from wires and beads, an abacus allows people to make calculations faster than simply using their own brains.

That's the same principle behind modern-day computers. Abacuses remained the fastest calculators available until the seventeenth century. In some places around the world, people still use these devices.

Scientists and mathematicians designed more modern and mechanical calculators in the seventeenth and eighteenth centuries. But neither the abacus nor the early mechanical calculators can be considered computers. Why not?

While these devices make it easier and faster for people to do math, they need people to operate them for every calculation. Computers are machines that can operate automatically.

In the nineteenth century, a British mathematics professor named Charles Babbage (1791–1871) designed something called the Analytical Engine. This design laid the basic framework for modern-day computers.

programmable: able to be given instructions for the automatic performance of a task.

binary: a math system that uses only the numbers 0 and 1.

WORDS TO KNOW

WHAT HAS WHEELS AND FLIES, BUT IS NOT AN AIRCRAFT?

A garbage truck.

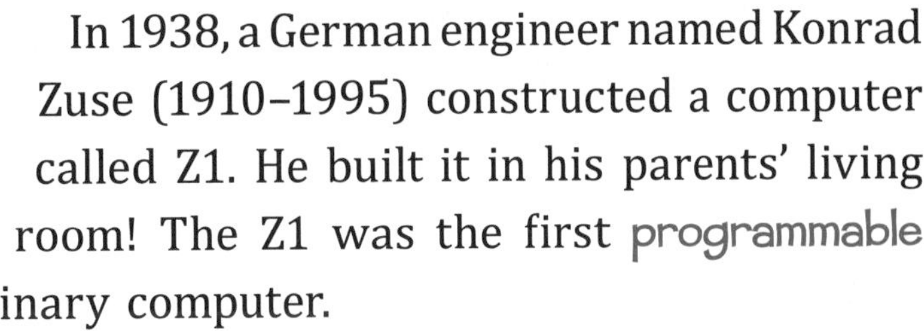

In 1938, a German engineer named Konrad Zuse (1910–1995) constructed a computer called Z1. He built it in his parents' living room! The Z1 was the first programmable binary computer.

Binary code is a system that uses the digits 0 and 1 to represent letters, numbers, and other characters in a computer. This code is a language that computers understand.

HELLO, ADA!

As a young girl, Ada Lovelace (1815–1852) showed a gift for mathematics. Back in the early 1800s, it was unusual for girls to study science and math. But Lovelace enjoyed the challenge. She worked with Charles Babbage, helping him to improve the design of his Analytical Engine. In fact, Babbage said, "She seems to understand it better than I do, and is far, far better at explaining it." Lovelace came up with a theory for how Babbage's engine could repeat a series of instructions. Many people now consider Lovelace the world's first computer programmer.

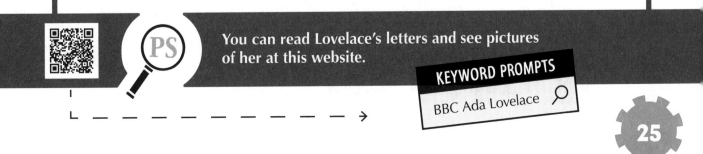

You can read Lovelace's letters and see pictures of her at this website.

KEYWORD PROMPTS

BBC Ada Lovelace

After all, computers do not speak the languages humans use to communicate, such as English or Spanish. Instead, people use code to write directions the computer can understand so it completes the tasks it's told to do.

Since their early days, computers have gotten smaller and faster. Early electronic computers were as big as large rooms and used huge amounts of electricity.

Today, we have small, lightweight laptop computers that weigh less than a bunch of bananas! We can even carry computers in our pockets. Cell phones and MP3 players are also computers.

WHEELS

Cars have them. Bicycles have them. Wagons have them. What are we talking about? Wheels! Thousands of years ago, someone used their knowledge about how wheels roll to create a tool that made it easier to get from place to place.

You might think of technology as being about only computers, but remember, technology is using scientific knowledge to solve problems. Technology is what people use to help them succeed in the environments where they live.

Wheels are one of the most important inventions in history. They are essential for transportation, of course. But people have also used them for many other purposes. For example, people who make pottery use wheels to create things out of clay.

Morse code: a code in which letters are represented by combinations of dots and dashes, or long and short signals of light or sound.

braille: a form of written language for blind people in which letters are represented by raised dots that are felt with the fingertips.

telegraph: an electric system or device for sending messages by a code over wires.

WORDS TO KNOW

BINARY CODES

Morse code and **braille** are both examples of binary codes. Morse code is a system of dots and dashes. These dots and dashes represent letters of the alphabet. In the past, people sent messages over **telegraph** lines using Morse code. Braille involves raised bumps that represent letters of the alphabet. Many blind people use these bumps to read with their fingertips.

You can translate messages into Morse code at this website! Try sending a secret message to a friend!

KEYWORD PROMPTS

Morse code translator

pottery wheel: a device that has a rotating disc on which clay is shaped by hand into bowls, pots, and other objects.

Mesopotamia: an ancient civilization located between the Tigris and Euphrates Rivers, in what is today part of Iraq.

BCE: put after a date, BCE stands for Before Common Era and counts years down to zero. CE stands for Common Era and counts years up from zero. This book was published in 2017 CE.

chariot: a two-wheeled, horse-drawn vehicle from ancient times, which was used in battle and in races.

spokes: wire rods or bars that connect the center of a wheel to its outer rim.

WORDS TO KNOW

Some early pottery wheels from Mesopotamia are as old as 3500 BCE. This is 300 years before people used wheels to travel in their chariots!

Early wheels looked very different from the ones we see on cars and bikes today. While many of today's wheels are made of rubber, the ancient ones were made of wood. Early wheels were solid. It wasn't until 2000 BCE that people developed wheels with spokes.

You might wonder what spokes do for a wheel. A spoked wheel can be built just as strong as a solid wheel. But the spoked wheel weighs much less than a solid one. Why does this matter? Imagine riding a bike with heavy, solid wheels. Do you think you could pedal as fast as you can on a modern-day bicycle?

DID YOU KNOW?

When it's completed in 2017, the Dubai Eye will be the world's largest Ferris wheel. It will stand about 853 feet high. One spin around the wheel will take about 48 minutes!

axle: a rod, pole, or bar on which a wheel rotates.

rotate: to turn around a fixed point.

efficient: wasting as little energy as possible.

energy: the ability or power to do work or cause change.

WORDS TO KNOW

Wheels are only one part of what makes a car travel quickly. Picture a car. It has pairs of wheels connected by axles. The wheels rotate around the axles. If they are placed correctly, wheels spin in an even circle around an axle. When wheels and axles are working efficiently, it takes little energy to move the car forward.

Computers and wheels are two examples of technology that we use every day. Can you think of other examples? Do you listen to a radio in the car? Do you rely on an alarm clock to wake you up in the morning? Technology is all around us! A makerspace is a terrific place to learn more about technology through projects and experiments. What new technology can you come up with?

CONSIDER AND DISCUSS

It's time to consider and discuss: How can technology and the engineering design process benefit us in solving problems in our daily lives?

PROJECT!

CREATE A BINARY CODE BRACELET

There are lots of ways to explore technology in a makerspace! Binary code is used to program computers. See if you can write the letters of your name as binary code. Instead of using the numbers 0 and 1, you'll use two colors of beads. Have fun!

SUPPLIES

- paper
- pen or pencil
- 2 colors of beads (three if you want spaces between the letters in your name)
- elastic or string for beads
- tape
- jewelry clasp (optional)

1 Using the chart on page 31, write down each letter of your name as a series of ones and zeros. For example, A would look like 01000001.

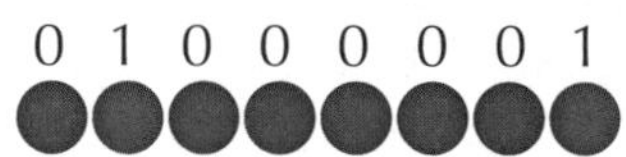

2 Choose one color bead for the number one and another color bead for zero.

3 On a flat surface, lay out the beads representing each letter in order until you have spelled your entire first name.

4 Cut a piece of string to 12 inches long. If you want to make a necklace with your last name too, you can cut the string longer. Place a piece of tape at one end of the string so your beads don't fall off as you put them on.

PROJECT!

5 Place each letter of your name's beads in order on the string. You can use a third color of bead to act as a space between each letter.

6 When you have finished, either use tape or a jewelry clasp to complete your binary coded bracelet! If you have elastic jewelry string, you can tie off the bracelet as long as it is easy to take on and off.

THINK ABOUT IT: How else could you use this binary code? What other materials could you use to create a binary message for someone?

TRY THIS! Try another coding exercise. Make a bracelet for a friend that has a secret message written in beaded binary code!

Letter	Binary Code
A	01000001
B	01000010
C	01000011
D	01000100
E	01000101
F	01000110
G	01000111
H	01001000
I	01001001
J	01001010
K	01001011
L	01001100
M	01001101
N	01001110
O	01001111
P	01010000
Q	01010001
R	01010010
S	01010011
T	01010100
U	01010101
V	01010110
W	01010111
X	01011000
Y	01011001
Z	01011010
space	00100000

PROJECT!

DESIGN A SPEEDY CAR

Kids around the globe make toy cars from whatever materials are available. Some move slowly, while others speed along. Not all designs are equally efficient. Using supplies you have on hand, see if you can make a fast car. Use the engineering design process to organize your work.

Caution: Ask an adult to help you poke holes in the box or container.

SUPPLIES

* small cardboard box or plastic container for car body
* pen or pencil
* scissors
* hole punch (optional)
* thin sticks, straws, bamboo skewers, or pencils for axles
* spools of thread, sewing bobbins, or tin foil for wheels
* rubber bands or paper clips
* tape or glue

1 Find a small cardboard box or plastic container to use as your car's body. If you have other materials you'd like to use for the car, go for it!

2 Using a pen or pencil, mark two holes directly across from each other on opposite sides of the car body. You'll want two holes near the front of the car. Repeat this process and mark two holes opposite each other near the back of the car.

3 Using scissors or a hole punch, cut out these axle holes from the car body. Ask an adult to help you!

4 Slip one axle through the two holes in the front of the car. Place the second axle through the back two holes.

PROJECT!

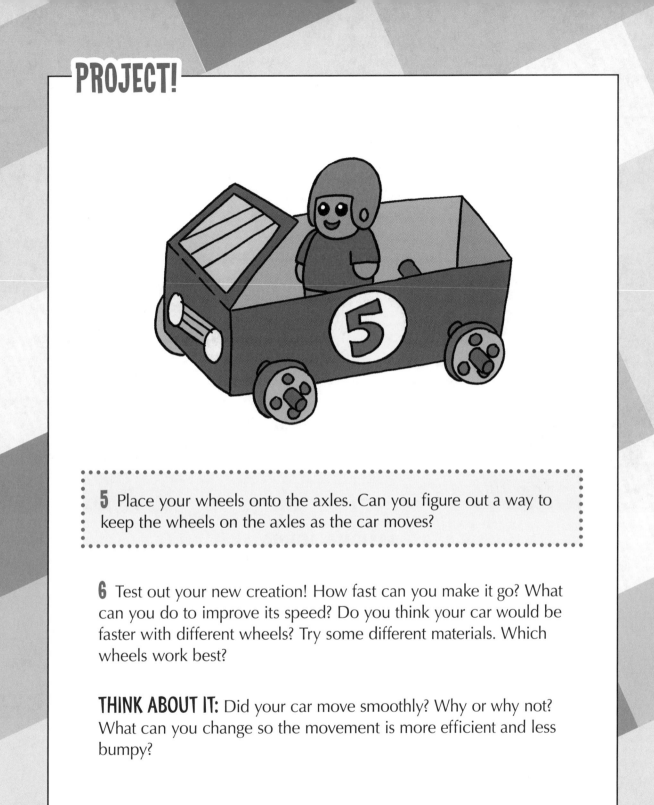

5 Place your wheels onto the axles. Can you figure out a way to keep the wheels on the axles as the car moves?

6 Test out your new creation! How fast can you make it go? What can you do to improve its speed? Do you think your car would be faster with different wheels? Try some different materials. Which wheels work best?

THINK ABOUT IT: Did your car move smoothly? Why or why not? What can you change so the movement is more efficient and less bumpy?

CHAPTER 3

MAKING MUSIC

You might listen to music on the radio in your bedroom or in the car. You might hear music playing in the grocery store or at a restaurant. Sometimes, teachers use music in classrooms and homeschools.

Music comes in many different styles. Classical, jazz, rap—there's a type of music to please just about everyone! What's your favorite music?

INVESTIGATE!

What kinds of instruments do you have in your own body? What kinds of sounds can you make using your body and materials from your makerspace?

A makerspace is a great place to work with materials to find ways of making music. Maybe you'll design a tube that makes a sound when you blow air through it. Maybe you will discover a certain noise that strings create when they're plucked. How else might you make music in your makerspace?

From the ancient Greeks to modern-day rock bands, all musicians are makers. They create new musical styles, songs, and even different instruments.

sound: the energy of vibration, which causes the sensation of hearing.

vibrate: to move back and forth or side to side very quickly.

particle: a very small piece of matter.

sound wave: an invisible vibration in the air that you hear as sound.

WORDS TO KNOW

THE SCIENCE OF SOUND

Music is made up of combinations of sounds. Where do sounds come from? How do sounds get from where they are made to your ears? Sound is a form of energy that is produced when things vibrate.

What happens when you bang on a drum? The tight material on the top of the drum vibrates very fast. This vibration causes air particles near the drum to vibrate, too. They bump into each other and cause the air particles around them to bump into other air particles. This continued bumping is called a sound wave.

medium: a substance, such as air or water, through which energy moves.

substance: the material that something is made of.

archaeologist: a person who studies ancient people through the objects they left behind.

WORDS TO KNOW

If your friend is playing a drum all the way across the room, can you feel those air particles next to the drum bumping around? The vibrations travel through a medium, such as air or water. Air is the medium for most sounds you hear, from a cat meowing to the telephone ringing.

Eventually, the sound wave from the drum travels as far as your ears, and the air inside your ears starts to vibrate. That's when you start to sense the vibrating drum as a sound.

DID YOU KNOW?

Your ears pick up sound while you sleep but your brain doesn't "hear" it.

The human ear is a terrific catcher of sound waves. Why? The curvy shape of your ears is great for funneling sound waves into your ear canal. As the sound waves hit your eardrum, your eardrum vibrates. These vibrations are passed on to your inner ear and make it possible for you to hear all kinds of sounds.

WOOLY MAMMOTH BAND

Archaeologists have discovered musical instruments in Ukraine dating back to 18,000 BCE. Guess what these ancient flutes were made from? The bones of a wooly mammoth! Talk about using materials you have on hand! Do you think early humans played music for the same reasons we play music today? What other purpose could music have had back then?

WHAT KIND OF MUSIC
ARE BALLOONS SCARED OF?
Pop music.

Sound waves do not travel forever. If they did, you could hear people shouting on the other side of the world! Sound waves lose energy and weaken as time passes.

Sound waves can also weaken because of obstacles in their way as they travel. If you are standing on the other side of the wall from where your friend is playing the drum, the sound will be quieter.

The Vegetable Orchestra, based in Austria, plays instruments made only from vegetables and fruits! Leek violins, pumpkin drums, and carrot flutes are just a few examples. **Take a look!**

pitch: the lowness or highness of a sound.

wavelength: the spacing of sound waves measured by the distance from the high point of one wave to the high point of the next wave.

frequency: how often something happens.

Hertz: a unit of frequency, equal to one cycle per second.

WORDS TO KNOW

PITCH

What's the difference between the rumble of a garbage truck and the squawk of a parrot? What makes some sounds low and others high?

The sound that an object makes changes based on how fast it's vibrating. If an object is vibrating quickly, it creates a high-pitched sound. If an object is vibrating more slowly, it will create a low-pitched sound.

Pitch is the lowness or highness of a sound. Pitch is created by sound waves that have either shorter or longer wavelengths. The shorter the wavelength, the higher the pitch. The longer the wavelength, the lower the pitch.

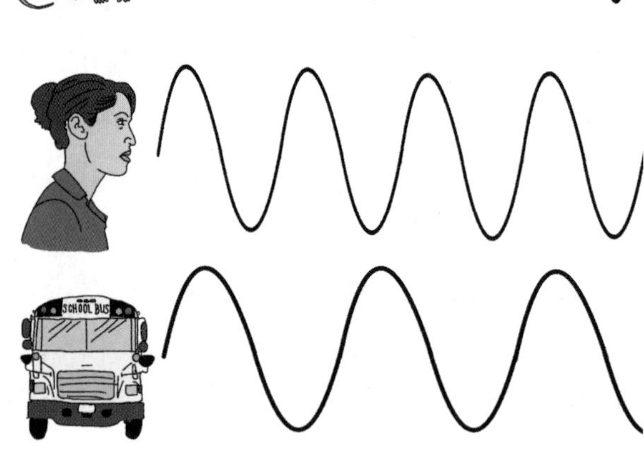

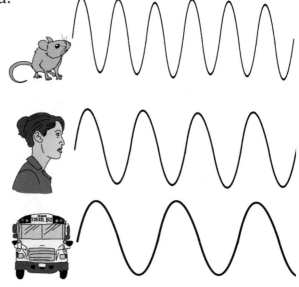

Scientists measure pitch by the number of wavelengths that travel through the air each second. They measure the frequency of sound waves with a unit called Hertz (Hz). People are able to hear sounds with frequencies ranging from around 20 Hz to 20,000 Hz. However, humans can best hear sounds from 1,000 to 5,000 Hz.

MUSICAL INSTRUMENTS

Do you play a musical instrument? There are many different kinds of instruments, including flutes, drums, and xylophones. Some, such as the drums and the triangle, are called percussion instruments. Others, including the flute and clarinet, are wind instruments. String instruments include everything from guitars to violins to giant basses.

Humans have been creating music with musical instruments for many thousands of years. Ancient Egyptians played harps and flutes. The ancient Greeks invented a water-powered pipe organ more than 2,200 years ago. It was known as a hydraulis. In cultures where Buddhism is the main religion, bells and drums have long been important musical instruments.

percussion instrument: describes a musical instrument played either by striking with the hand or with a handheld or pedal-operated beater, or by shaking.

wind instrument: a musical instrument sounded by wind or breath.

string instrument: a musical instrument that creates sound through vibrating strings or wires.

Buddhism: one of the world's major religions, based on the teachings of Buddha.

WORDS TO KNOW

DID YOU KNOW?

Even before birth, babies can hear music from inside their mom's bodies.

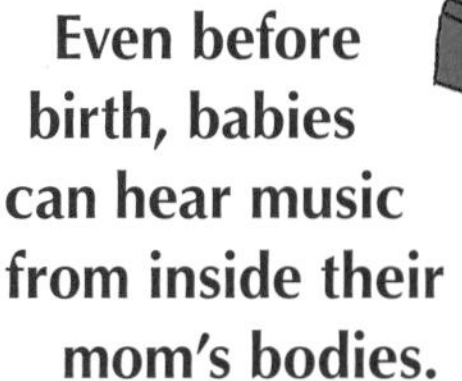
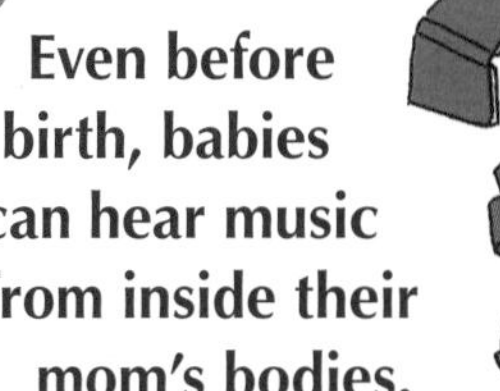
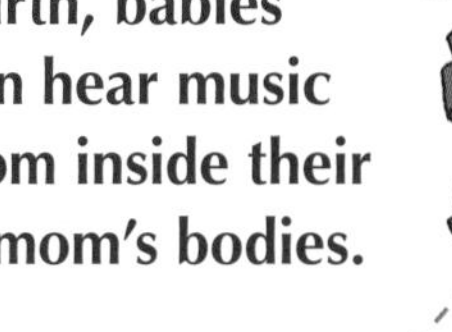

tropical: a hot climate, usually near the equator.

stalactite: a cave formation that looks like an icicle hanging from the ceiling.

WORDS TO KNOW

Drums in Africa might not look the same as drums in the United States or Europe. Why? Instrument makers in different parts of the world have their own ideas about what they want their instruments to look and sound like. Also, the materials available to people are often different from one place to another.

People in Arctic regions far in the north have used bone, skin, and stone to build their instruments. Those living in tropical regions might make instruments from bamboo, wood, reed, and so on. What materials do you have near you that can be used to make a musical instrument?

CONSIDER AND DISCUSS

It's time to consider and discuss: What kinds of instruments do you have in your own body? What kinds of sounds can you make using your body and materials from your makerspace?

In the next chapter, we'll learn more about art, clothing styles, and different decorating projects you can try out in your makerspace!

MUSIC IN NATURE

In Virginia's Luray Caverns is one of the world's most unusual musical instruments. The Great Stalacpipe Organ is located inside a cave and was designed and built in the 1950s by electrical scientist and mathematician Leland W. Sprinkle. How does it work? An electric console causes rubber mallets to strike ancient stalactites of different sizes within the cave, producing a variety of sounds or musical notes. When someone plays the organ's keyboard, the whole underground landscape turns into a musical instrument!

PROJECT!

MAKING MUSIC WITH WATER

SUPPLIES

- 4 to 8 water glasses
- water
- metal spoon or other metal utensil

Different sounds have different pitches because of the sizes of their wavelengths. You can hear the difference using a few simple materials in your makerspace!

1 Fill each of your glasses with a different amount of water. Be sure that one has only a little bit of water in it and that another is nearly full.

2 Lightly tap each glass with your metal utensil. Be careful not to tap too hard.

3 Make some music! Did the fuller glasses have higher or lower pitches than the glasses with less water? Why? How else can you change the sound coming from these water glasses?

TRY THIS! Take one of the glasses that is barely filled and add a little water to it at a time. After each addition, gently tap the glass with your utensil. How does the pitch change? What does that tell you about wavelengths?

PROJECT!

DESIGN A DRUM

SUPPLIES

* coffee can or other empty cylindrical container
* masking or electrical tape
* construction paper
* markers or crayons
* stickers (optional)
* 2 pencils or pens (optional)
* tissue paper (optional)

People have been making and using drums for thousands of years. Sometimes, they use them for communication. Other times, they use them to make music. Design and make your own drum to use for whatever purpose you like!

1 Collect all your materials. Place strips of tape over the open top of the container in a crisscross pattern. Keep adding tape strips until the container is completely covered. Since this tape surface will be the top of the drum, make sure that it is firm.

2 Decorate your drum. Wrap a piece of construction paper around the can. Cut away any excess paper and tape it in place You can color or add stickers to the construction paper to make your drum look great.

3 For each drumstick, crumple a piece of tissue paper into a ball shape. Place this tissue paper ball onto the pointed end of your pen or pencil. Wrap tape around the tissue ball so that it is securely attached to the pen or pencil. Repeat for the second drumstick.

4 Make some music with your new drum! How can you vary the sounds you make? Can you beat out a familiar tune?

TRY THIS! Make another drum from a different-sized container. How does the pitch change in a drum that is a different size?

PROJECT!

CREATE A COMPLETELY NEW MUSICAL INSTRUMENT

A fun part of being a maker is coming up with new ideas. In this activity, you will design and construct a brand-new instrument. Use the engineering design process to get organized. There is no limit to what materials you can use—here are some suggestions to get you started. What sound will your instrument make?

SUPPLIES

- pencil and paper
- strings or elastics
- wood scraps
- dried beans or rice
- recycled containers
- tape or glue
- cardboard
- any other materials you can think of!

1 Brainstorm about the kind of instrument you might like to make. It can have strings, be a percussion instrument, a noisemaker, a wind instrument, or something never seen before. Look around your makerspace to see what materials might be fun to use for your instrument. Sketch your design on a sheet of paper.

2 Start building your instrument. If something isn't working, try a different design. Can you get the sound you want? Are you surprised by the sounds you do get? How can you improve your design?

THINK ABOUT IT: Does your instrument have a high or low pitch? How can you change this? What other instruments can you make to go along with your first instrument?

DID YOU KNOW?

A young Russian inventor created an electronic instrument called a theremin, where the player can change its pitch and volume just by moving his or her hands near the instrument's two antennae.

PROJECT!

MAKE A SOUND AMPLIFIER

Ever wish you could hear the sound on a cell phone better? Sometimes, the volume seems too quiet even when you have it turned up all the way. Here's a simple solution. You can make your own amplifier.

SUPPLIES

* pen or marker
* cardboard toilet paper tube
* scissors
* 2 plastic cups
* glue
* cell phone

1 With your pen, trace the bottom edge of a cell phone onto the middle of the cardboard toilet paper tube. Be sure to trace all the way around the phone so you have a little rectangle shape.

2 Use scissors to cut out the rectangle you have just traced. Be careful not to cut all the way though both sides of the tube.

3 Trace the end of your toilet paper tube onto one side of a plastic cup. This will give you a circle shape. Do the same thing in about the same spot of the other plastic cup. Again, be careful not to cut through both sides of your plastic cup.

4 Place one end of the cardboard tube into the hole in one of the plastic cups. Put the other end of the cardboard tube into the hole in the other cup.

WORDS TO KNOW

amplifier: a device that increases the strength or power of sounds.

PROJECT!

5 Squeeze a layer of glue all the way around the edges where the cups and the tube meet. This will keep the tube in place and prevent any sound from escaping through the circles you cut in the cups.

6 Once the glue is dry, insert the phone into the slot you made in the cardboard tube. Be sure to leave a little open space in the tube so that you don't block any of the holes/speakers on your phone. See what happens when you play music or use the speakers on the phone.

THINGS TO DISCUSS: Did the sound get louder with the amplifier? Why do you think this is the case?

CHAPTER 4

AMAZING ART

Humans have created many kinds of artwork through the ages, from ancient cave paintings to electronic pieces of art that light up and make sound! Everyone has different ideas of what art looks like, what it's used for, and what it's made of.

One thing all art has in common is that it's made with materials. What kind of art materials do you have in your makerspace? Do you have paint, markers, string, clay, and paper? All of these things can be used to make art.

INVESTIGATE!

Does art have a purpose or is it simply something humans enjoy doing and looking at?

No one is sure exactly when people first started creating art. Some scholars believe that people have been making art as far back as 100,000 years ago or more. This prehistoric art came in many forms. In Indonesia, researchers have discovered geometric patterns carved onto shells. Cave paintings have been found in places ranging from Asia to Europe to Australia.

ARTISTS AS MAKERS

When you think of art, what comes to your mind? Some people might say paintings. Others might mention sculpture. Mobiles and collages are also art. These are all forms of art you can make in your makerspace!

Just like you, prehistoric artists were makers. They couldn't drive to an art supply store for paints, brushes, or canvas. Instead, they used the materials that were handy. Cave painters might have used charcoal or soot from a fire for the color black. The color yellow came from ochre. Brown and red pigments came from clay.

prehistoric: before written history.

geometric: a style of art that uses simple shapes, such as lines, circles, and squares.

sculpture: the art of making two- or three-dimensional representations of forms, especially by carving wood or stone or by casting metal or plaster.

mobile: a construction or sculpture made of shapes that can be set in motion.

collage: artwork made by gluing pieces of different materials to a flat surface.

ochre: an iron ore that is usually red or yellow.

pigment: a substance that gives something its color.

WORDS TO KNOW

extinct: when a group of plants or animals dies out and there are no more left in the world.

portrait: a picture of a person, especially one showing only the face or head and shoulders.

WORDS TO KNOW

Early artists also made sculptures from whatever materials were available. Many African artists used wood to sculpt, but insects and the weather often damaged these artworks through time. Other African sculptors created their masterpieces in stone. These creations were stronger and longer lasting.

Much like today's artists, ancient artists painted all kinds of images. They painted the outlines of human hands. They painted animals that the artists saw around them. Some of these animals, such as the giant kangaroo of Australia, have gone extinct since the paintings were made. We can learn a lot about history and the lives of ancient people through their art.

Why do people create art? Sometimes, people use art to communicate their feelings. Other times, people make art to document events or to capture moments in time.

For example, painters have created portraits of kings, queens, and other important people for many centuries. These portraits tell viewers about the styles of clothing people used to wear. They also let viewers know that the person in the painting was important.

WHAT DID THE ARTIST DRAW BEFORE SHE WENT TO BED?
The curtains.

DRESSING UP

Throughout history, many people have not had lots of clothes. They might have a work outfit and a set of clothes for when they went someplace nice. Have you ever heard the expression, "Sunday best?" This refers to a person's best clothes, something they might wear for a special occasion.

Do you dress up in costumes on Halloween? Many cultures around the globe have ceremonies, rituals, or holidays that require special costumes.

ceremony: a formal public or religious occasion, usually one celebrating a particular event or anniversary.

ritual: a series of actions or behaviors regularly followed by someone, often as part of a ceremony.

tapestry: a heavy cloth with pictures or designs woven into it, used especially as a wall hanging.

WORDS TO KNOW

IMPROVE YOUR ROOM

Artists through the ages have created artwork to decorate living spaces or important buildings, such as castles or churches. Have you ever seen a stained-glass window? That's artwork designed to make a space more beautiful. Restaurants and coffee shops often display artwork on their walls. Does your school have bulletin boards in the hallways that display student artwork? Your local public library or town hall might have paintings or tapestries lining its walls.

PS A STAINED GLASS WINDOW MADE IN 1884

Carnival: a time of public merrymaking in certain cultures, involving music, processions, dancing, and masks.

sequins: small pieces of shiny plastic or metal used as an ornament, especially on clothing.

elaborate: made with much detail or great care.

headdress: a covering or ornament for the head, particularly one worn for ceremonies.

WORDS TO KNOW

In the countries where people celebrate a festival called Carnival, dancers wear costumes covered with feathers, sequins, and other colorful details. In Venice, Italy, people celebrating Carnival often wear detailed masks and costumes that are considered to be works of art. For Chinese New Year, some folks wear elaborate clothing, headdresses, or even a dragon costume for dancing in parades!

MAKE A FRIEND

What's something that most kids love? Stuffed animals! Some stuffed animals come from fancy toy shops. Others are made by hand.

If you've ever read any of the Little House books by Laura Ingalls Wilder, you know that the characters in the book did not have expensive, store-bought toys. They made their own dolls from materials they had on hand, such as corncobs and fabric scraps.

A German company named Steiff was the first business to make stuffed animals, starting in 1880. This company made stuffed elephants, monkeys, donkeys, camels, cats, and more.

It wasn't until 1902 that Steiff made the first teddy bear. Ever since, bears have been one of the most popular kinds of stuffed animals around.

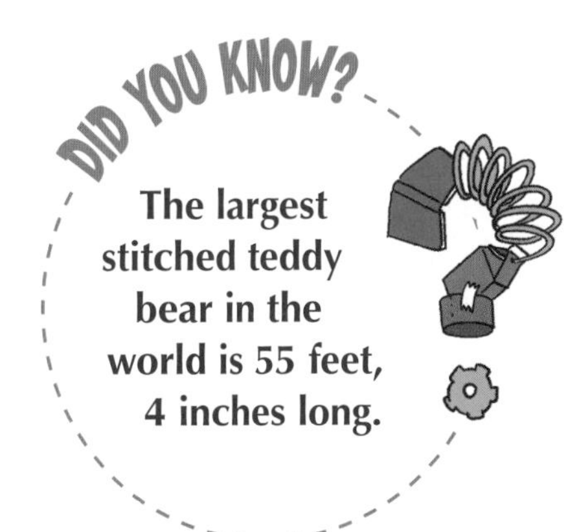

DID YOU KNOW?
The largest stitched teddy bear in the world is 55 feet, 4 inches long.

Stuffed animals can be made of many different materials—felt, fabric, stuffing, even fake fur. Makers through the decades have created stuffed animals with sewing machines or just a needle and thread.

Art is a wonderful way to experience the world. So is science! In the next chapter, we'll learn more about different science experiments you can do in your makerspace!

CONSIDER AND DISCUSS

It's time to consider and discuss: Does art have a purpose or is it simply something humans enjoy doing and looking at?

PROJECT!

MAKE A TROPICAL BIRD MASK

Masks have long been a way for people to dress up and pretend to be someone, or something, else! In this activity, you will create a fancy bird mask from simple materials in your makerspace. You'll be the coolest bird in the forest. Squawk!

You can see different beak templates here.

KEYWORD PROMPTS

bird mask template

SUPPLIES

- 5 to 6 paper plates
- pencil or pen
- glue
- scissors
- paintbrush
- crayons or markers
- colored tissue paper
- hole punch (optional)
- string

1 Draw eyes on a paper plate. If the plates are thin, glue two together. Use scissors to cut the eyes out.

2 Use a brush to lightly coat the plate with glue. Cover the plate with tissue paper. Cut the tissue paper off of the eye holes.

3 Brush another coat of glue over the tissue paper and let the plate dry.

PROJECT!

4 Fold another paper plate in half. Cut this plate to the size and shape you'd like the beak to be. Cover this beak with tissue paper and glue (as with the mask) and let dry.

5 Use glue or packing tape to attach the beak to the mask.

6 Draw and cut feathers from the other paper plates. Color them whatever colors you like and attach them to the edges of your mask. What else can you make feathers out of?

7 Punch a hole in each side of the mask. Tie a string to each side, then tie around your head. You're ready to go!

TRY THIS! If you want to create a complete costume, you can dress in clothes that are the same colors as the feathers on your mask. What else can you add to your outfit to make it more birdlike?

Take a look at some of the masks and costumes worn during Carnival in Venice, Italy!

KEYWORD PROMPTS

Carnival masks Venice video

PROJECT!

DESIGN A MAGIC WAND

Wizards, magicians, and gods often have magic wands as part of their toolkits. The Greek god Hermes carried a magic wand known as a caduceus. And, of course, Harry Potter and the students at Hogwarts all have their own magic wands. Create your own fantastic wand!

SUPPLIES

- 1 stick, about 10 to 14 inches long
- yarn
- glue
- colored tissue paper
- glitter
- marble

1 With your yarn, tie a knot near one end of the stick. Be sure the knot is tight so the yarn doesn't slip off.

2 Wind yarn all the way up to the other end of the stick. The yarn doesn't need to cover every bit of space on the stick. It can be spaced out. Tie another knot at the opposite end. Cut the yarn if still attached to a larger ball.

3 Cover the yarn and the stick with glue. Wrap your colored tissue paper around the stick so it's covered.

4 Brush glue over all of the tissue paper. While the tissue paper is still wet with glue, sprinkle it with glitter.

5 Glue a marble to one end of your wand. Let the wand dry and you're ready for battle!

TRY THIS! Can you create another magic wand using different materials? What about a magic wand that can be folded into a pocket?

PROJECT!

CREATE A SUNCATCHER

Suncatchers are decorations that catch the light from the sun. Some are made of crystals or stained glass. In this activity, you'll make a suncatcher from plastic you find in the recycling bin. You can find some templates for your suncatcher here.

SUPPLIES

* pen or pencil
* paper
* clear plastic packaging
* marker
* colored tissue paper
* glue
* pin or needle
* string

1 Draw the suncatcher design onto a sheet of paper.

2 Place a piece of clear plastic on top of the paper with the design on it. Use the marker to trace the design onto the plastic.

3 Cut the excess plastic off so you are left with the shape of your design.

4 Cut out a variety of little pieces of different colored tissue paper. Glue these pieces of tissue to the plastic.

5 Near the top of your suncatcher, make a hole using a pin or needle. Thread a piece of string through the hole. Hang up your creation in a sunny spot and enjoy!

THINK ABOUT IT: What other materials could you use to make a suncatcher that allows light to pass though it?

PROJECT!

MAKE A MOBILE

You might have seen a mobile hanging over a baby's crib. Mobiles are also used as wind chimes to make lovely sounds when the wind blows. There are many ways to design a mobile. In this activity, you will make a mobile designed for indoors.

SUPPLIES

* cardboard
* scissors
* ruler or measuring tape
* beads, buttons
* paint
* glitter or glitter glue
* construction paper or cardstock
* hole punch
* string, yarn, or fishing wire
* glue

1 Cut a strip of cardboard that is about 12 inches around. Cut a smaller circle out of the middle of the card circle. This will be the loop at the top of the mobile. Decorate your cardboard hoop.

2 Use a hole punch to cut a hole every 3 inches or so around your cardboard hoop. You will make eight holes in all.

3 Cut eight pieces of string each about 2 feet long. Tie a piece of string through each hole in the hoop so that most of the string hangs down.

4 Cut eight more pieces of string that are 18 inches long. Put these strings through the same holes as before but have these strings pointing up on top of the hoop. Pull the ends of these eight strings together and make a knot. About 2 inches below that knot, tie one more knot. This will make a loop to hang your mobile from when it's done.

PROJECT!

5 Add beads, buttons, or paper designs (with holes punched in) to the longer strings that are hanging downward. Be careful not to choose anything too heavy or your mobile might lean to one side. Tie a knot at the bottom of each string when you have completed it. It's okay for the strings to be different lengths if you like.

6 Hang up and enjoy your creation!

TRY THIS! Make a themed mobile. For a soccer mobile, you might make balls out of paper, then make mini jerseys. Or, make a mobile where everything is your favorite color.

PROJECT!

CREATE YOUR OWN STUFFED ANIMAL

Stuffed animals come in all shapes and sizes. Try to come up with a design you've never seen before. You'll also improve your sewing skills in this activity.

Caution: Ask an adult to help with the pins and needle.

SUPPLIES

- scissors
- 1 square foot fabric
- chalk
- markers
- pins
- dull #6 needle
- thread
- stuffing or cotton balls

1 After designing your animal or shape, fold your piece of fabric in half. Using chalk or markers, draw the outline of your design into the fabric. It is a good idea to keep your design simple.

2 Cut out the shape, adding an extra ½ inch or so around the edges. Be sure to keep the two halves of your fabric together while cutting. You may want to pin them together before cutting.

3 Measure a length of thread from the tip of your left shoulder to the tip of the fingers on your right hand. Thread your needle. Make a knot on one end.

4 Push your needle up through the bottom layer of fabric and then through the top layer. Pull the thread all the way through until the knot is touching the bottom layer of fabric. For the next stitch, put the tip of your needle about ½ an inch to the right of your first stitch. Pull through both layers of fabric again. Repeat this stitch technique until you are three quarters of the way around your design. Turn the fabric inside out.

PROJECT!

5 When you have only a couple of inches left of unstitched fabric, stuff your animal with stuffing or cotton balls. Finish sewing until there are no gaps in the edge of your animal. Draw a face on your animal, if desired. Enjoy your new buddy!

THINK ABOUT IT: Was your design easy to turn into a stuffed animal? Can you think of ways to make a fancier animal in the future? What other materials can you use?

SEWING SAFETY

Sewing can be fun, but it involves tools that you need to use with care. Practice sewing on a scrap piece of fabric before using your final materials. You always want to keep the sharp end of a needle away from your face. Also, when taking the needle in and out of the fabric, be careful not to poke your fingers! And ask for help if you need it. That's how everyone learns!

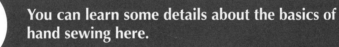

You can learn some details about the basics of hand sewing here.

CHAPTER 5

SUPER-COOL SCIENCE

What comes to mind when you think of a scientist? You might imagine someone working in a lab, wearing a white coat. You might picture your science teacher setting up activities in your classroom. Your makerspace is another great place to do some science!

Scientists ask questions and conduct experiments to learn about the natural world. You can be a scientist, too! Use your senses to observe the world around you and ask questions about what you notice. Being a scientist is fun!

INVESTIGATE!

What would the world be like without buoyancy and gravity?

BUOYANCY

Water is one of the most important substances on Earth. People need it to survive. In fact, up to 60 percent of the average adult's body is made of water. When babies are born, their bodies are a whopping 78 percent water! In addition to drinking water, humans use water for bathing and for swimming.

force: a push or pull applied to an object.

buoyancy: a force that allows an object to float in liquid.

displace: to cause something to move from its usual or proper place.

WORDS TO KNOW

You've probably noticed that some objects sink in water while others float. This has to do with a force called buoyancy. Buoyancy is how a body rises, or floats, when it's in a fluid. If you toss a wooden stick into a body of water, it floats. But if you toss a stone into the water, it sinks. Do you float or sink when you're in the water? Why? And who figured out why this happens?

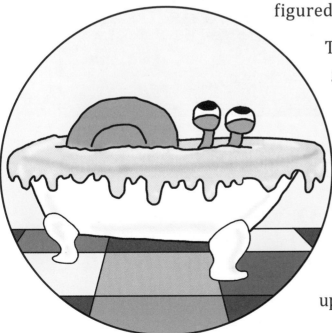

To understand buoyancy, let's go back to ancient Greece, where a mathematician named Archimedes was taking a bath. When he got into the tub, some water was displaced and it spilled over the rim of the tub. Why did this happen? And who was going to clean up the mess?

Now, while some folks would just make sure not to fill their tub so high the next time, Archimedes was a true scientist. He was curious. He investigated and asked questions. He noticed that a large object displaces more water than a small object.

Archimedes figured out that if the weight of the object placed in the water is less than the weight of the water being displaced, the object will float. If the weight of the object placed in the water is more than the weight of the water being displaced, the object will sink. Today, we refer to this as the Archimedes' principle, or buoyancy.

SHIPS AND BUOYANCY

When you think about buoyancy, what comes to mind? Many people might say boats, canoes, rafts, ships, or kayaks. All of these float. Even if early explorers didn't know the science, buoyancy has been important to people since they started to travel by water.

People have built wooden sailing vessels in many shapes and sizes. Europeans built logboats about 9,000 years ago. Wooden sailing ships were used in Mesopotamia and ancient Egypt as far back as 3500 BCE. By 1100 CE, large wooden ships were being built in China. These were capable of carrying heavy loads of cargo. Around the world, people still make ships of wood.

cargo: the goods transported in a ship, vehicle, or airplane.

hull: the main body of the ship that includes the bottom, sides, and deck.

mass: the amount of matter in an object.

WORDS TO KNOW

DID YOU KNOW?

The *Syrakosia* was a three-masted royal ship measuring about 230 feet long. It was built in Greece around 240 BCE.

Have you ever seen a huge cruise ship? Why don't these enormous ships sink? After all, they are made of metal and they are loaded with people and cargo. Metal ships can remain lighter than the amount of water they displace because they aren't completely solid. The ship's hull is hollow. The hull adds support to the ship without adding mass.

gravity: a force that pulls objects toward each other, and all objects to the earth.

universe: all existing space and matter, considered as a whole.

WORDS TO KNOW

Is there a limit to how much weight a ship can carry before it is not buoyant anymore? Yes. The weight of the ship cannot increase past the amount of water it displaces. Otherwise, the ship won't be buoyant anymore. And nobody wants to ride on a ship that sinks!

GRAVITY

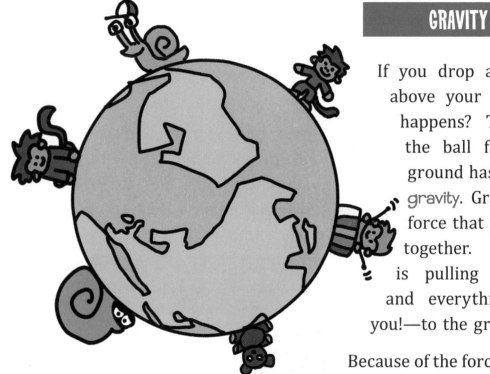

If you drop a ball from above your head, what happens? The reason the ball falls to the ground has to do with gravity. Gravity is the force that pulls things together. The earth is pulling the ball—and everything around you!—to the ground.

Because of the force of gravity, people, animals, trees, buildings, and even the air are held on Earth. There is also gravity in space. All of the stars, moons, and planets in the universe have gravity, too. In fact, every object has gravity. Even your own body has gravity. But we don't notice it because the force of Earth's gravity is much stronger.

WHY DID THE TEACHER JUMP INTO THE LAKE?

She wanted to test the water!

Have you ever stepped on a scale to see how much you weigh? Your weight, or how many pounds you are, is actually a measurement of the force of gravity on your body! Your weight shows just how hard gravity is pulling you to Earth's surface.

Throughout history, scientists have designed many experiments trying to learn more about gravity. Galileo Galilei (1564–1642) was an Italian scientist. There is a story about Galileo dropping balls from the Leaning Tower of Pisa. The balls were said to be made of the same material, but they had different masses. Galileo wanted to prove that these two objects, when dropped at the same time, would reach the ground at the same time. By experimenting, he found this to be true. Can you do this experiment in your makerspace?

YOUR CHANGING WEIGHT

A person who weighs 100 pounds on Earth would weigh only 38 pounds on Mars. This is because Mars has lower gravity than our planet does. The same 100-pound person would weigh 236.4 pounds on Jupiter because Jupiter has a higher gravity than Earth. And on the sun, a 100-pound person would weigh a whopping 2,707 pounds—that's more than a ton!

You can figure out your weight on other planets using the tool at this website.

liquid: a substance that flows freely, such as water and oil.

viscosity: the state of being thick and flowing slowly.

property: a quality or feature of something. The way something is.

WORDS TO KNOW

VISCOSITY

Imagine a cup filled with a thick milkshake and another cup filled with water. What happens when you tip the two cups upside down? Do the liquids flow out of the cups at the same speed?

Viscosity is a property of liquids. It describes how slowly or quickly a liquid flows. Scientists talk about liquids as having high or low viscosity. A thick milkshake has high viscosity and flows slowly. Water has low viscosity and flows quickly.

Peanut butter, honey, and glue are some other substances that are viscous. They flow very slowly. What else do you know about these sticky substances? Are there any uses for viscous materials? Can you think of other viscous liquids?

Scientists have explored the natural world for as long as people have been curious. In the next chapter, we'll find out more about games around the world and through history. Then you can create new games in your makerspace!

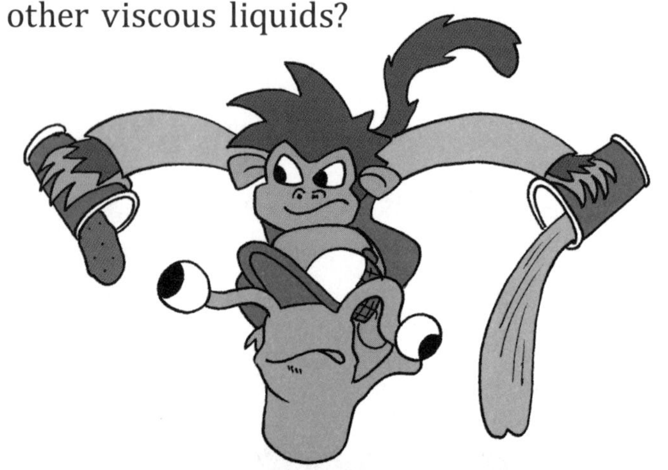

CONSIDER AND DISCUSS

It's time to consider and discuss: What would the world be like without buoyancy and gravity?

PROJECT!

DESIGN A BOAT THAT FLOATS

Throughout history, boats have come in a variety of shapes and sizes. In your makerspace, try to design one that floats and can carry some cargo. Use the engineering design process to organize your work.

SUPPLIES

* paper
* pencil or pen
* clay
* aluminum foil
* popsicle or craft sticks
* wood scraps
* scissors
* glue or tape (optional)
* bathtub or sink
* rocks or other weight

1 Brainstorm some designs for your boat. It could be anything from a canoe to a raft to a sailing ship. Sketch your ideas on a piece of paper.

2 Using whatever materials you have handy, build your boat. If any parts of your boat need gluing, you should let the glue dry before trying the boat out.

3 Place your boat into a sink or tub at least partially filled with water. Ship ahoy!

4 Can your ship carry weight? Add some weight to the boat and see if it still floats. How much weight does it take to sink your ship?

5 Redesign your boat to carry more weight and test out your redesign. How does it work?

TRY THIS! How can you make your boat move? Is your boat design as speedy as you'd like? If not, what could you do to improve how fast it moves? What different materials might help?

PROJECT!

FRUIT THAT FLOATS

Some objects float and are buoyant. Others sink and are not buoyant. Try this activity to discover more about the buoyancy of fruit.

SUPPLIES

* tall vase or large bowl
* water
* pieces of fruit, including oranges, apples, and bananas

1 Pour water into the container to about three-quarters full. Place the orange (with its peel on) into the water.

2 After you see what happens in Step #1, take the orange out of the water. Peel the orange and place it back into the water. What happens? Record your observations in your engineering notebook.

3 Try the same experiment with other fruit, such as bananas and apples, to see which ones float with and without their skin. What happens?

4 Use the peel from the orange to surround a small weight, such as a little stone. Does the peel help it stay afloat?

WHAT'S HAPPENING? The peel does something very important for the fruit in terms of buoyancy! The peel helps displace enough water to make the orange buoyant. It also contains lots of tiny air pockets. These pockets make the unpeeled orange less dense than the water. So, the unpeeled orange floats. When you take the peel off, the orange doesn't displace enough water to overcome gravity. Because the peeled orange is denser than the water it displaces, it sinks.

PROJECT!

GROSS GOOP!

In this activity, you will combine water, glue, and borax and observe what happens to their consistency as they are mixed.

Caution: Have an adult help with the borax. Wear eye protection when handling.

SUPPLIES

- eye protection
- medium-sized bowl
- water
- white glue
- stirrer
- food coloring (optional)
- borax
- Ziploc bag

1 In a bowl, mix ½ cup water with 1 ounce of glue (about a quarter of an average school glue bottle.) If you want colored goop, add a few drops of food coloring to the water and glue mixture. Stir the mixture. Lift a little of this solution out of the bowl with your stirrer. What happens?

2 Add ¼ cup borax to the glue and water mixture. Stir this slowly. Lift a little of this mixture out of the bowl and see how its consistency has changed.

3 Stir the mixture as much as you can with the stirrer. Then use your hands to knead the mixture until it becomes less sticky. This will be messy, but kneading helps the mixture bond completely. If there's any water left in the bowl, just pour it out. Now play with your goop!

4 Store your goop in a plastic bag in the refrigerator so it doesn't grow mold. Make sure to wash your hands after handling the goop.

THINK ABOUT IT: How did the consistency of the goop change over the course of this activity?

PROJECT!

MAKE A PARACHUTE

Parachutes slow down objects that are falling toward the ground. They do this by increasing the air resistance as the object falls, thus slowing down the effects of gravity. Which kind of bag makes the best parachute? How much weight can the parachute carry?

SUPPLIES

* paper plate
* plastic shopping bags
* marker
* scissors
* tape
* hole punch
* yarn or string
* paper cup
* pennies or marbles or a small action figure

1 Place the plate on one side of the plastic bag. Use your marker to trace the outline of the plate onto the bag. Cut out the circle.

2 Make four dots on the plastic circle, one at the top, bottom, and at each side. Try to have the dots about equal distances apart from one another.

3 Put a piece of tape over each dot. Use a hole punch to make a hole at each dot. The hole will go through the tape and the bag.

4 Cut four pieces of yarn or string about 10 to 12 inches in length. Attach one piece of string to each of the holes.

5 Make four holes around the top edge of the paper cup. Again, they should be about the same distance apart. Attach one piece of string to each hole in the cup. Place a small action figure or some pennies or marbles into the cup.

PROJECT!

6 Find a place to drop your parachute where it can get some height—from a tall staircase, the top of a jungle gym, or somewhere else. Let your parachute fly! Did your parachute hit the ground fast or float in the air for a while? What happens if you add more weight to the cup?

TRY THIS! Now make another parachute using a heavier-weight plastic bag. You could also try a very lightweight piece of fabric. How does that change your results? Record your observations in your engineering notebook.

BE GALILEO

You can recreate Galileo's famous experiment in your makerspace. Gather a few balls of different weights and sizes. Perhaps you could use a tennis ball, ping-pong ball, football, and basketball. Stand on a chair—be careful! Stretch your arms wide. Hold one ball, each of a different size, in each hand. Drop the two balls at the same time. What happens? Why? The force of gravity that's acting on the balls is the same, even though the balls have different weights. Does one ball hit before the other? What else might have an affect on the balls? How about a feather and a bowling ball? Will those two objects fall at the same rate? Why?

Find out in this video!

KEYWORD PROMPTS

bowling ball feather video

PROJECT!

EGG DROP CHALLENGE

An egg will break if you drop it from a height unless it is somehow cushioned. In this activity, you will design a container that will protect an egg when you drop it from 8 feet.

Caution: Make sure that your egg can't splatter anything.

SUPPLIES

- paper
- pencil
- 3 to 4 eggs
- 15 straws
- 10 popsicle sticks
- 40 inches of tape
- measuring tape
- an old rag or towel for cleanup

1 Use the engineering design process to get started. Brainstorm in your engineering notebook some possible designs for a container. It needs to protect your egg from breaking when dropped from 8 feet high.

2 Using only the specified amounts of straws, popsicle sticks, and tape, build your egg container. What can you do to protect the egg? Think about both the inside and outside of the container!

3 Using the measuring tape, determine where 8 feet high is.

4 Place an egg in your container and drop it. What happens? Did your egg container work or did your egg break? If the egg broke, how could you improve the design to better protect the egg inside? Does your egg stay in one piece if dropped from 10 feet high?

TRY THIS! Try this egg drop challenge again using materials other than straws, popsicle sticks, and tape. What other materials might work better? Try out your new designs. Did your egg break?

CHAPTER 6

GREAT GAMES

People play games for fun! There are board games, ball games, card games, and many other varieties. Some games, such as solitaire, can be played on your own. Other games, including dodgeball, can involve a large group of players. A makerspace can be a great place to play games, as well as to design them!

People have played games for a very long time. Even when getting food took up most of their daylight hours, people still managed to squeak in some time to play games. In fact, people had board games before they had written language!

INVESTIGATE!

Why do people play games? Do people play games today for the same reasons they played them in ancient times?

token: an object used in a game that serves as a sign or symbol.

pawn: a game piece with the smallest value and size.

decipher: to convert a text written in code or an unknown language into understandable language.

WORDS TO KNOW

ANCIENT GAMES

Archaeologists recently found elaborate game pieces in a burial mound located in southeast Turkey. Some of the game pieces look like dogs, pigs, and even pyramids. This game also included dice and circular **tokens** made from white shell and black stone. Some of the game pieces were painted in different colors. These game pieces are about 5,000 years old!

The Royal Game of Ur is an ancient game. This is a race game where players throw their dice to move their **pawns** toward the goal. The oldest known sets of this game are about 4,800 years old. Archaeologists found the Royal Game of Ur in southern Iraq. Players used seven markers, one set of black and one set of white, as well as three, four-sided dice.

THE ROYAL GAME OF UR

The Royal Game of Ur is the oldest-known board game for which we still have the original rules! Irving Finkel (1951–), a man who worked for the British Museum, figured out the rules by **deciphering** them from stone tablets.

grid: a network of lines that cross each other to form a series of squares or rectangles.

objective: a goal of an action, as in a game.

WORDS TO KNOW

Ancient Egypt is known for a game called senet. The senet board is a grid of 30 squares, which are arranged into three rows of 10 squares. The game includes two sets of pawns. Each player typically had five to seven pieces in his or her set.

DID YOU KNOW?

A set of the Royal Game of Ur was found in the tomb of ancient Egyptian pharaoh Tutankhamen.

Historians have had to make educated guesses about the rules for how to play senet, since the original rules have been lost. Most people agree that the objective of the game is to race one's pieces across the board. Instead of dice, senet players threw sticks.

Illustrations of people playing this game have been found in ancient Egyptian tombs. Some players believed that winners of this game would be protected by the gods. Senet boards were often buried with people, along with other objects they might need in the afterlife.

THIS ANCIENT SENET GAME IS FROM 1300s BCE. THE NAME OF A PHARAOH, AMENHOTEP III, IS CARVED ON THE SIDE.
CREDIT: BROOKLYN MUSEUM

Middle Ages: the period of European history from about 350 to 1400 CE.

Renaissance: the period of European history from the 1300s to the 1600s, which is marked by a flourishing of literature and art.

strategy: a careful plan or method.

WORDS TO KNOW

People continued to create new games. Some were made of fancy materials and stored in special cases. Other games were drawn in the dirt or on animal skins. Dice could be made from practically any material. Archaeologists have found dice made of brass, marble, copper, glass, ivory, and even animal bones! Dice from ancient Rome often had six sides, similar to most dice we use today.

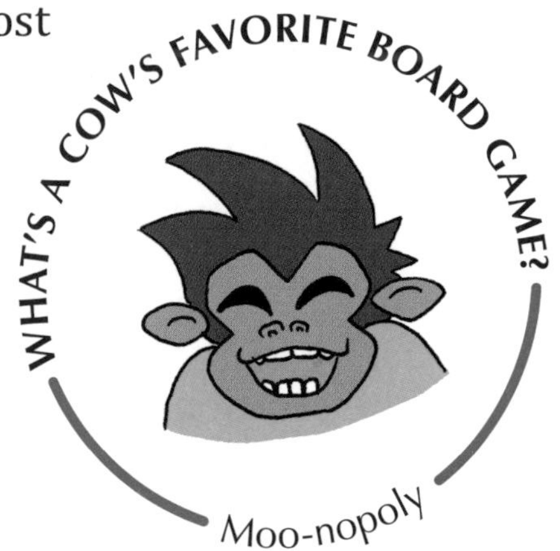

WHAT'S A COW'S FAVORITE BOARD GAME?
Moo-nopoly

In ancient cultures, board games were mainly played by adults. For example, during the Middle Ages and the Renaissance, people used the game of chess to teach the strategies of war. But after a while, children got into the board game craze, and that's still true.

PLAY MANCALA!

From Africa to Asia to the Caribbean, people have been playing mancala for thousands of years. You might be surprised to find out that some ancient board games can be played on computers today!

Try playing the game mancala at this website. **See if you can beat the computer!**

MAKING A GAME

Ready to try some gamemaking in your makerspace? Even though there are more games around the world than you could probably count, the best ones all have a few things in common.

DID YOU KNOW?

In 2016, the largest Monopoly board ever was assembled in the Netherlands. It measured 9,690 square feet.

Each game has its own purpose and rules. If the game and its rules aren't clear, it can be frustrating for players. Games often have actions that the players must follow to participate.

Some games, such as dice games, might just be about luck. Other games, including Scrabble, involve strategy or skill. And some are a mixture of strategy and luck—think Monopoly!

Just as engineers make prototypes of rockets or computers, so do people designing games. For a game prototype to be a success, the rules must be clear. There shouldn't be so many playing pieces that it is confusing.

Players must know the objective of the game from the beginning. They must also understand how to keep score. The first run-through of any game might not work out. But just like engineers, game designers keep redesigning until their games can be played smoothly all the way from start to finish.

DID YOU KNOW?

If you have access to a makerspace, you could design your own game board with wood or other materials. A 3-D printer is a great resource for creating plastic playing pieces.

Every year, engineers and scientists design and test new structures, from giant bridges to super-fast spacecraft. Musicians and artists create instruments, symphonies, costumes, and artwork of all kinds. And new games and toys are always fun and welcome.

What invention will engineers create next? What brilliant new painting or sculpture will people line up to see 200 years from now? No one can be sure, but perhaps you will come up with an amazing creation in your brand new makerspace!

CONSIDER AND DISCUSS

It's time to consider and discuss: Why do people play games? Do people play games today for the same reasons they played them in ancient times?

PROJECT!

MAKE A NEW-BUT-OLD GAME

You probably have a bunch of games at home that you've played a million times. What about some that you no longer use? Why not mix things up and make your own new-but-old game?

Note: Ask for permission before you mix up pieces between games and remember to put them back when you are done.

SUPPLIES

- at least one already existing board game
- cardboard or poster paper
- markers or crayons
- pen or pencil
- paper
- small objects to use as new playing pieces

1 Choose a game or two that you already own. Do you want to use its board? If not, you can create a brand-new game board using the cardboard or poster paper and crayons or markers.

2 Are there any game pieces you want to use in your new game? You could swap the pieces from one game to another. You can also use little objects as pieces, such as action figures or coins.

3 There are many ways to change an existing game. For example, you could change how many times you must go around the board. Or take away or add time limits.

4 Make a set of directions, writing out the rules for your new game so other players can know how to play.

5 Do a trial run of the game, playing with friends or family members. Do your directions work? Does someone win? What can you change to make the new game easier to play?

PROJECT!

BUILD A GAME TIMER

Many games have timers to keep track of how long certain steps in the game take. Can you design and create a timer that measures 10 seconds? Use the engineering design process to get started.

SUPPLIES

- stopwatch
- small water or soda bottles
- sand or water
- pebbles
- rice
- rubber bands
- duct tape (or strong packing tape)
- plastic wrap
- scissors
- paper clips
- pencil and paper

1 Think about the basic problem you want to solve. In your engineering notebook, sketch out some possible designs for your timer.

2 Choose one of your designs and start building a prototype of it with materials on the list.

3 When you have completed your prototype, test it out against a stopwatch. Does your timer measure 10 seconds? If your timer is either longer or shorter than 10 seconds, see if you can tinker with your design to adjust the time.

4 Can you make another timer that measures 20 seconds? 40 seconds? What are the limits to your timer?

TRY THIS! See if you can make a second timer using different materials. You could try plastic tubing, cardboard tubes, or whatever else you think might work.

DID YOU KNOW?

Some historians believe that Roman soldiers played the game of hopscotch while wearing their heavy armor. They did this to keep fit!

WORDS TO KNOW

armor: a covering, often made of metal, that protects the body in battle.

PROJECT!

CREATE A NEW OUTDOOR BALL GAME

Just about every ball game involves rules. In this activity, you will create your own ball game. Use the engineering design process to get started. Have fun!

SUPPLIES

* pen or pencil
* paper
* chalk
* an outdoor ball of any size
* several players

1 Brainstorm about all the ball games you have ever played outside. For each game, think about the following: the size of the ball used, the rules of the game, the size and shape of the area where this game is played, and the number of players. Are there any other things about ball games that you can think of?

2 In your engineering notebook, come up with a name for your game and a list of rules. Draw the area shape you will need to play. For example, a hopscotch game requires blocks in a certain pattern. What will your game need?

3 Ask an adult if you can go outside to use the chalk and draw the game design on the ground. Don't forget to bring your ball!

4 After setting up the game area, explain the rules to the people who will be trying your new game.

TRY THIS! Can you think of a variation on your newly invented game that would include two balls instead of one? How would the rules change?

PROJECT!

GLOSSARY GAME

Use words from the text and the glossary to create a silly story.

- **noun:** a person, place, or thing
- **plural noun:** more than one person, place, or thing
- **adjective:** a word that describes a noun
- **verb:** an action word
- **adverb:** a word that describes a verb

Out-of-This-World Adventures

______ (NOUN-NAME) was an engineer from ______ (NOUN-PLACE). She was ______ (ADJECTIVE) than anyone. She traveled around the city of ______ (NOUN-PLACE) in a ______ (ADJECTIVE) ______ (NOUN). But she was always searching for ______ (ADJECTIVE) forms of transportation and ideas for ______ (ADJECTIVE) buildings. One day, she heard about a ______ (ADJECTIVE) skyscraper made of ______ (NOUN). She had to see it for herself! The clever engineer packed ______ (NOUN), ______ (NOUN), and ______ (NOUN) in her suitcase. She filled a spaceship's fuel tank with ______ (ADJECTIVE) ______ (NOUN). ROAR! The engines sprang to life! She was on her way to the planet ______ (NOUN-NAME).

When the engineer arrived, she ______ (VERB) the rocketship's ______ (ADJECTIVE) door. There was no gravity! She ______ (VERB) and ______ (VERB) all over the place. She saw buildings made of ______ (ADJECTIVE) ______ (NOUN). Finally, she arrived in the center of a ______ (ADJECTIVE) city. The planet's beings traveled around in ______ (ADJECTIVE) ______ (NOUN). After searching for a while, she found the ______ (ADJECTIVE) skyscraper she was looking for! It was ______ (ADJECTIVE)! There were elevators that ______ (VERB). And windows made of ______ (NOUN). On every floor was a ______ (ADJECTIVE) ______ (NOUN). She took tons of photos of this ______ (ADJECTIVE) structure before heading back to Earth. This ______ (ADJECTIVE) engineer couldn't wait to make a similar skyscraper at home.

A

abacus: an instrument for performing calculations by sliding beads along rods.

amplifier: a device that increases the strength or power of sounds.

archaeologist: a person who studies ancient people through the objects they left behind.

architecture: the style or look of a building.

armor: a covering, often made of metal, that protects the body in battle.

automatic: working with little or no direct control by people.

axle: a rod, pole, or bar on which a wheel rotates.

B

BCE: put after a date, BCE stands for Before Common Era and counts years down to zero. CE stands for Common Era and counts years up from zero. This book was published in 2017 CE.

binary: a math system that uses only the numbers 0 and 1.

braille: a form of written language for blind people in which letters are represented by raised dots that are felt with the fingertips.

bridge: a structure built over something, such as a river or road, so that people can cross.

Buddhism: one of the world's major religions, based on the teachings of Buddha.

buoyancy: a force that allows an object to float in liquid.

C

calculation: a mathematical determination of the number or size of something.

cargo: the goods transported in a ship, vehicle, or airplane.

Carnival: a time of public merrymaking in certain cultures, involving music, processions, dancing, and masks.

ceremony: a formal public or religious occasion, usually one celebrating a particular event or anniversary.

chariot: a two-wheeled, horse-drawn vehicle from ancient times, which was used in battle and in races.

climate: the weather patterns in an area during a long period of time.

collaborate: to work with others.

collage: artwork made by gluing pieces of different materials to a flat surface.

collapse: to fall in or down suddenly.

computer: an electronic device that stores and processes information.

concept: an idea.

D

data: information in the form of facts and numbers.

decipher: to convert a text written in code or an unknown language into understandable language.

dense: how tightly the matter in an object is packed.

design: to make a sketch or plan.

device: a piece of equipment, such as a phone, that is made for a specific purpose.

digital art: art created using computers.

displace: to cause something to move from its usual or proper place.

DIY: do-it-yourself.

E

efficient: wasting as little energy as possible.

elaborate: made with much detail or great care.

energy: the ability or power to do work or cause change.

engineer: a person who uses science, math, and creativity to design and build things.

engineering: the use of science and math in the design and construction of machines and structures.

extinct: when a group of plants or animals dies out and there are no more left in the world.

F

force: a push or pull applied to an object.

frequency: how often something happens.

G

geometric: a style of art that uses simple shapes, such as lines, circles, and squares.

gravity: a force that pulls objects toward each other, and all objects to the earth.

grid: a network of lines that cross each other to form a series of squares or rectangles.

H

headdress: a covering or ornament for the head, particularly one worn for ceremonies.

Hertz: a unit of frequency, equal to one cycle per second.

hull: the main body of the ship that includes the bottom, sides, and deck.

I

ice dam: a wall of ice that forms on the edge of a roof that can cause water damage.

Inca: the South American people who built a great empire in the Andes Mountains 800 years ago.

invention: an original process or device.

L

laser: a device that generates an intense beam of light. Lasers are often used in cutting and drilling, playing CDs, and even for surgery.

liquid: a substance that flows freely, such as water and oil.

M

makerspace: a work space inside a library, school, or other place where people can work together to make, explore, and learn using tools of all kinds.

mass: the amount of matter in an object.

matter: anything that has weight and takes up space.

medium: a substance, such as air or water, through which energy moves.

Mesopotamia: an ancient civilization located between the Tigris and Euphrates Rivers, in what is today part of Iraq.

method: a way to do something.

Middle Ages: the period of European history from about 350 to 1400 CE.

milling machine: a machine that can cut or carve different materials.

mobile: a construction or sculpture made of shapes that can be set in motion.

Morse code: a code in which letters are represented by combinations of dots and dashes, or long and short signals of light or sound.

O

objective: a goal of an action, as in a game.

obstacle: something that blocks a person's way or stops progress.

ochre: an iron ore that is usually red or yellow.

P

particle: a very small piece of matter.

pawn: a game piece with the smallest value and size.

percussion instrument: describes a musical instrument played either by striking with the hand or with a handheld or pedal-operated beater, or by shaking.

pigment: a substance that gives something its color.

pitch: the steepness of a slope, particularly of a roof. Also the lowness or highness of a sound.

portrait: a picture of a person, especially one showing only the face or head and shoulders.

pottery wheel: a device that has a rotating disc on which clay is shaped by hand into bowls, pots, and other objects.

prehistoric: before written history.

principle: the basic way that something works.

programmable: able to be given instructions for the automatic performance of a task.

programming: to give a computer a set of step-by-step instructions that tells it what to do.

property: a quality or feature of something. The way something is.

prototype: a working model that lets engineers test their idea.

R

ravine: a small narrow valley with steep sides.

Renaissance: the period of European history from the 1300s to the 1600s, which is marked by a flourishing of literature and art.

ritual: a series of actions or behaviors regularly followed by someone, often as part of a ceremony.

rotate: to turn around a fixed point.

S

sculpture: the art of making two- or three-dimensional representations of forms, especially by carving wood or stone or by casting metal or plaster.

sequins: small pieces of shiny plastic or metal used as an ornament, especially on clothing.

shingles: rectangular tiles that cover a roof or the sides of a building. Shingles can be made of wood, metal, asphalt, or other material.

sloped: a surface that has one end or side that is at a higher level than the other.

sod: the grass-covered surface of the ground.

sound: the energy of vibration, which causes the sensation of hearing.

sound wave: an invisible vibration in the air that you hear as sound.

spokes: wire rods or bars that connect the center of a wheel to its outer rim.

stalactite: a cave formation that looks like an icicle hanging from the ceiling.

strategy: a careful plan or method.

string instrument: a musical instrument that creates sound through vibrating strings or wires.

structure: something that is built, such as a building, bridge, tunnel, tower, or dam.

substance: the material that something is made of.

suspension bridge: a bridge that has its roadway suspended from two or more cables that are strongly anchored at the ends.

system: a group of objects or parts that work together.

T

tapestry: a heavy cloth with pictures or designs woven into it, used especially as a wall hanging.

technology: the tools, methods, and systems used to solve a problem or do work.

telegraph: an electric system or device for sending messages by a code over wires.

thatch: a plant material, such as straw, used to cover the roofs of buildings.

tinker: to adjust or repair something in an experimental manner.

token: an object used in a game that serves as a sign or symbol.

tropical: a hot climate, usually near the equator.

U

universe: all existing space and matter, considered as a whole.

V

vibrate: to move back and forth or side to side very quickly.

viscosity: the state of being thick and flowing slowly.

W

wavelength: the spacing of sound waves measured by the distance from the high point of one wave to the high point of the next wave.

wind instrument: a musical instrument sounded by wind or breath.

METRIC CONVERSIONS

Use this chart to find the metric equivalents to the English measurements in this book. If you need to know a half measurement, divide by two. If you need to know twice the measurement, multiply by two. How do you find a quarter measurement? How do you find three times the measurement?

English	Metric
1 inch	2.5 centimeters
1 foot	30.5 centimeters
1 yard	0.9 meter
1 mile	1.6 kilometers
1 pound	0.5 kilogram
1 teaspoon	5 milliliters
1 tablespoon	15 milliliters
1 cup	237 milliliters

BOOKS

Awesome Paper Projects You Can Create. Ventura, Marne. Capstone Press, 2015.

Fun Things to Do with Cardboard Tubes. Ventura, Marne. Capstone Press, 2014.

I Can Make Decorations (Makerspace Projects). Reid, Emily. Windmill Books, 2015.

Maker Lab: 28 Super Cool Projects. Challoner, Jack. DK Children, 2016.

Maker Projects for Kids Who Love Paper Engineering (Be A Maker!). Sjonger, Rebecca. Crabtree Publishing Company, 2016.

Maker Projects for Kids Who Love Music (Be A Maker!). Sjonger, Rebecca. Crabtree Publishing Company, 2016.

Maker Projects for Kids Who Love Robotics (Be A Maker!). Bow, James. Crabtree Publishing Company, 2016.

Mini Science Fun (Mini Makers). Felix, Rebecca. Lerner Publications, 2017.

Starting a Makerspace. Williams, Pam. Cherry Lake Publishing, 2017.

3-D Engineering: Design and Build Your Own Prototypes. May, Vicki V. Nomad Press, 2015.

WEBSITES

Crafts for Kids – PBS Parents website: pbs.org/parents/crafts-for-kids/category/learning/sensory

DIY – Instrument Maker website: diy.org/skills/instrumentmaker

Engineer Girl website: engineergirl.org/4356.aspx

Mister Maker – Kids ABC website: abc.net.au/abcforkids/makeanddo/craft/show.htm?show=MISTER-MAKER

Science Toy Maker website: sciencetoymaker.org

Tinker Lab website: tinkerlab.com

Toilet Paper Roll Crafts – DLTK website: dltk-kids.com/type/tp_roll.htm

***Zoom* – PBS Kids website:** pbskids.org/zoom/activities/sci

QR CODE GLOSSARY

Page 4: instructables.com/id/Create-a-Maker-Space-for-Kids

page 25: bbc.com/news/science-environment-34243042

page 27: morsecode.scphillips.com/translator.html

page 37: vegetableorchestra.org/index.php

page 52: assets.marthastewart.com/styles/wmax-520-highdpi/d29/msl_1009_0910_birdmask2_image/msl_1009_0910_birdmask2_image_xl.jpg?itok=YuGsLAzJ

page 52: o.aolcdn.com/smp/is/uploads/wordpress/uploads/2015/10/flamingo-head-template-01.png

page 52: 4.bp.blogspot.com/-RtcSGIxvVdg/VIB8NZgw0xI/AAAAAAABcFA/9ZQloe71DFA/s1600/111-how-to-draw-beak-easy-steps-4.png

page 53: theculturetrip.com/europe/italy/articles/the-carnival-of-venice-and-its-traditional-masks

page 55: firstpalette.com/tool_box/printables/star-6inch.pdf

page 55: s-media-cache-ak0.pinimg.com/originals/5b/3d/dc/5b3ddca106b842721efee63778dbf1be.jpg

page 59: madeeveryday.com/2014/03/5-tips-for-teaching-your-child-to-hand-sew.html/

page 65: exploratorium.edu/ronh/weight

page 71: blogs.discovermagazine.com/d-brief/2014/11/06/watch-feather-bowling-ball-fall-speed/#.WSSHasm1uL8

page 76: play-mancala.com

ESSENTIAL QUESTIONS

Introduction: What problem do you see that you would like to fix? What can you invent to solve it?

Chapter 1: Why do engineers and designers strive to improve products used in our daily lives? Why do we use the engineering design process to solve design challenges?

Chapter 2: How can technology and the engineering design process benefit us in solving problems in our daily lives?

Chapter 3: What kinds of instruments do you have in your own body? What kinds of sounds can you make using your body and materials from your makerspace?

Chapter 4: Does art have a purpose or is it simply something humans enjoy doing and looking at?

Chapter 5: What would the world be like without buoyancy and gravity?

Chapter 6: Why do people play games? Do people play games today for the same reasons they played them in ancient times?